## Fight the Winter Blues

# Don't Be SAD

### *Your Guide*

### *to*

### *Conquering*

### *Seasonal Affective Disorder*

# Fight the Winter Blues

# Don't Be SAD

## *Your Guide*

## *to*

## *Conquering*

## *Seasonal Affective Disorder*

By Celeste A. Peters

Foreword by Dr. Chris Gorman

Script: Good Health Books

CALGARY

Published & distributed by Script Publishing Inc.
Suite 200, 839 - 5th Avenue S.W.
Calgary, Alberta, Canada T2P 3C8

# Table of Contents

# Foreword

THE EFFECT OF SEASONS ON ILLNESS HAS been observed since the time of Hippocrates, the father of medicine. As the seasons change, both climatic conditions and the number of daylight hours move through an annual cycle. Seasonal weather patterns generate numerous, obvious effects on health. Anyone who suffers from arthritis can attest to the pain brought on by cold, damp weather. But what about seasonal changes in the amount of sunlight we are exposed to? Can these affect human health as well?

Prior to 1979, it was believed that light did *not* have a biological effect on humans. This belief was based on studies that showed no behavioral or hormone level shifts in human experimental subjects exposed to the same intensities of light that animals respond to. In 1979, Dr. Alfred Lewy at the University of Oregon postulated that people may be less responsive to light than animals. Subtle light cues essential to the survival of animals go unheeded by humans. After all, we can buy a coat when winter approaches; animals have to grow one. Dr. Lewy exposed a group of people to higher intensities of light than previously tested. Lo and behold, their hormone levels shifted. Modern research into light therapy and its effect on humans was born.

Since then, scientific progress into understanding light and its effect on humans has proceeded at a rapid rate. Research centers in the United States and all over the world are investigating important questions.

What are the crucial wavelengths of light that mediate light's positive effect on mood? Which are the exact tracts in the brain that light works through? At the Foothills Hospital Mood Disorders Clinic in Calgary, Alberta, Canada, we have studied many patients with winter depression over the last seven years. One of our findings is that light treatment is safe in regard to the eye. Considering what is happening to the ozone layer, it may be safer to use artificial light with screens that eliminate potentially harmful ultraviolet rays than it is to go for a walk outside . . . a scary thought.

Dr. Raymond Lam, a leading researcher in seasonal affective disorder (SAD) at the University of British Columbia, has been working on the important eye mechanisms connected to the effect of light on patients with winter depression and on other treatments that may be helpful. Dr. Anthony Levitt from the Clarke Institute of Psychiatry in Toronto has also been instrumental in advancing the science of SAD research. His work with light visors has caused much discussion in this field, as it shows that all intensities of light from a visor are beneficial to SAD patients. These two researchers have helped put Canada on the map in a scientific community that continues to be fascinated with seasonal affective disorder. Many patients who previously suffered through years of debilitating depression with no hope of effective treatment are now living full lives because of their work.

That is why this book is important. It serves the purpose of informing patients and others about seasonal affective disorder and the exciting new therapies available to combat it. *Don't Be SAD* also helps to unveil the mystery of mood disorders, encouraging people apprehensive about seeking treatment to come forward and put their terrible depression behind them. If this book helps only one person to do that, all of the effort put into it will have been more than worthwhile.

Dr. Chris Gorman, B.M.Sc., M.D., F.R.C.P.(C)
Mood Disorders Clinic
Foothills Hospital

# Acknowledgments

THE HARD WORK AND VALUABLE ADVICE of numerous people made preparation of this book possible. I would especially like to thank Dr. Chris Gorman and Dr. Michael Terman for their generous donation of time and technical expertise in the field of SAD research. The excellent advice received from other researchers in the field is also greatly appreciated. Bev Whitmore supplied a great deal of the nutritional information in Chapter 11 and compiled the delicious, easy-to-prepare recipes located in Appendix B. Thanks Bev! Thanks are due Bruce Thorpe, who compiled and verified the names and addresses of the myriad of SAD researchers, clinicians, support organizations and light unit suppliers listed in the appendices. Kind and thoughtful input also has come from Leslie Demytruk, Joan Hoffos, Nancy Leishman, Janice McInulty, Joe Ronn, Michael Speraw, Ralph Sperry, Duncan Worthington and a host of wonderful people who shared their personal accounts and insights regarding SAD in the hope that others might benefit. My heartfelt thanks to all of you.

*Celeste A. Peters*
*Calgary*
*September 1994*

# PART 1

# Are You SAD?

# INTRODUCTION

**I**T'S A MISERABLE, COLD, DOWNRIGHT UGLY Saturday outside. Inside, you're moping around the house, looking for something, anything, to pique your interest and hold your attention for even a few minutes — some activity that won't take too much energy. You head for the kitchen and down three or four donuts while contemplating the situation. Hmmm . . . well, when all else fails, there is usually something worth watching on television. You click the remote. Cartoons on every channel? Oh, right. It's Saturday morning. The world belongs to children . . . young people . . . those of us over 20 don't count this morning. Come to think of it, do we count at all, at any time? What's the use? You struggle upstairs, hoping just a bit more shuteye will put a whole new slant on the day. Blah!

If the above scenario strikes a familiar chord — if you feel depressed, sleep a great deal, experience fatigue, have an irresistible urge to eat high-carbohydrate foods and sweets and perhaps even lose interest in sex for a prolonged period *at the same time every year* — you might be suffering from a medical syndrome known as "seasonal affective disorder" (SAD) or its milder manifestation, the seasonal blues.

It is the seasonality of this syndrome that, above all else, sets it apart from other mood disorders (see Glossary for a definition of "mood disorders"). SAD people succumb to prolonged bouts of depression and an assortment of concurrent symptoms at the same time almost every year. Some people feel they are at their worst during the summer months, but the majority of SAD people in Canada and the northern United States are depressed during the cold, short days of winter.

If you fit the most common profile of SAD sufferer, your symptoms begin to show up in the fall, sometime between September and November. They abate as spring arrives. You probably have what is commonly referred to as "winter SAD." You may be one of the many people who feel a growing sense of dread or depression around the autumnal equinox, when the hours of darkness exceed the hours of daylight. The shorter day becomes more pronounced when the clocks are turned back an hour in October and the sun suddenly sets much earlier in the evening. Your sense of panic might be subtle and subconscious or right out in the open.

If the symptoms you begin to experience at this time are annoying and somewhat debilitating but not severe

3

enough to seriously hinder your ability to function, you are going through a bout of the "winter blues," the milder form of winter SAD. The blues may become particularly bothersome by February, bringing on "cabin fever," that irresistible urge to escape your cooped-up winter household and flee to the wide open spaces of a sunny, milder climate.

> Good grief! Winter is coming again and bringing with it months of unbearable hopelessness, fatigue and weight gain.

There is also a summer version of SAD that has a slightly different set of symptoms. It is discussed in Chapter 3. Summer SAD is less common than winter SAD and its sufferers generally do not respond to light therapy. Why? Because this form of seasonal affective disorder appears to have a different underlying cause that has more to do with the heat and humidity of summer than the hours of daylight.

*Don't Be SAD* is designed to provide information to a wide range of readers.

• **If you suspect you have seasonal affective disorder:** do the self-assessment questionnaire in Chapter 1 before tackling the rest of the book. The symptoms of SAD affect different people in varying degrees of severity. Knowing whether you are seriously SAD or prone to the milder form of the syndrome, the winter blues, will help you focus on the appropriate course of treatment discussed in Part 3. You should find the suggested lifestyle changes in Chapters 11 to 14 particularly useful if you are blue. This same information will benefit seriously SAD people, but the most dramatic improvement in their symptoms will come about through the use of light therapy, medication and/or psychotherapy presented in Chapters 8, 9 and 10.

*Note: The self-assessment questionnaire is provided as a general guide. It is extremely important that you obtain a definitive diagnosis from your doctor if you suspect you are seriously SAD. **Do not self-diagnose**. As you will see, the symptoms associated with SAD are common to several other medical problems. You want to be certain you are treating the correct ailment.*

• **If you already have been diagnosed with SAD:** skip over the self-assessment. You and your doctor likely have SAD on the run with light therapy or medication. But are you aware of the exciting variety of light therapy equipment now available? Are you up-to-date on the latest medications, such as Zoloft, a close relative of Prozac that appears to have less potential to cause anxiety? If not, Chapters 8 and 9 should be of particular interest. Further along in Part 3, you will also find useful tips on how to adapt your diet, exercise routine and the "built" environment of your home and office to further minimize the impact of SAD on your life.

• **If you are a friend or family member of someone who suffers from SAD:** it can get pretty rough trying to cope with the emotional highs and lows SAD brings to a relationship. *Don't Be SAD* will help you better understand your partner's plight. In fact, Chapter 15 is addressed specifically to you. Discover when to push and when to back off in order to provide the loving support that is so essential while maintaining your own sense of perspective.

Some people like to delve into details. Others find it impossible to deal with graphs and numbers when they are depressed. With this in mind, material that is a bit more technical is presented separately throughout the book in sections titled "Clinically Speaking." These can be skipped over without loss. However, curiosity might draw you back to read them once your depression has lifted.

*Don't Be SAD* includes a wealth of personal accounts supplied by people affected with seasonal affective disorder who wished to share their stories. (Their true names have not been used in order to protect their privacy.) As you will see from their accounts, SAD comes in several degrees of strength, from the seasonal blues to severe clinical depression. The good news is, regardless of where you fit into the SAD spectrum, there is a lot you can do to put your life back on an even keel and keep it there. Whether you decide to try light therapy in your own home under the supervision of a doctor, seek professional counselling or simply modify your diet and exercise routine, there is help available.

## CHAPTER 1

# How SAD Are You?

**Y**OU SUSPECT YOU ARE SAD. OR MAYBE someone you live or work with is demonstrating many of the symptoms. *Don't Be SAD* is designed to do three things. First, it helps determine if you or someone close to you is either clinically SAD or perhaps suffering the seasonal blues. The self-assessment in this chapter gives you a pretty good indication. To have your suspicion confirmed, see your doctor. (More about this later.) Next, you receive a comprehensive overview of the various treatments that have proven effective against seasonal mood disorders, including the exciting non-invasive technique of light therapy. Finally, you are brought up to speed on the most recent research into SAD. Find out what is likely causing the seasonal roller coaster ride you are on! And don't overlook the important information in the appendices, which include lists of SAD clinics in cities throughout North America, support groups, "light box" suppliers and suggestions for further reading. Now, on to your self-assessment.

But first, I emphasize that there is no straightforward lab test that can determine if you have SAD. A more subjective means of diagnosis must be used. Fortunately, there are many easily identifiable symptoms associated with SAD. Their presence or absence at certain times of the year, combined with an assessment of their severity, makes it possible to get a good idea of whether or not you suffer from SAD. But keep in mind that a number of the symptoms associated with SAD beset everyone from time to time, and do not alone constitute a SAD affliction. The SAD syndrome includes symptoms common to several other syndromes and forms of mood disorder, so it is important to get a fix on whether you have SAD and, if so, to what extent you are in its grip.

In order to get as accurate a picture as possible of your situation, complete the following questionnaire **before** you read this book. All too often it is easy to exaggerate the presence or degree of your symptoms unintentionally after reading and empathizing with the material about to be discussed. Take the self-assessment quiz now, score yourself and then see what SAD is all about.

# SAD Self-Assessment

## Section 1: Seasonality Check

Think back at least two years into your past, farther if possible. Over this time period, can you identify months in which you regularly:

1. Felt better or worse than at other times of the year?

   Yes ☐  No ☐

2. Got out and socialized more or withdrew and shied away from social contact more than at other times of the year?

   Yes ☐  No ☐

3. Experienced a pronounced increase or decrease in appetite?

   Yes ☐  No ☐

4. Gained or lost weight?          Yes ☐  No ☐

5. Slept more than usual or experienced insomnia?

   Yes ☐  No ☐

6. Felt more energetic or more fatigued than at other times of the year?          Yes ☐  No ☐

7. Lost or gained interest in sex?          Yes ☐  No ☐

Did you answer yes to any of these seven questions? If so, fill in the chart provided on the next page. For each of the categories on the chart, put an "X" in the appropriate square under the month or months you normally experience these shifts in mood or behavior. Don't feel

## Seasonality of symptoms

|  | Jan. | Feb. | Mar. | Apr. | May | June | July | Aug. | Sept. | Oct. | Nov. | Dec. |
|---|---|---|---|---|---|---|---|---|---|---|---|---|
| 1. Feel your best | | | | | | | | | | | | |
| Feel your worst | | | | | | | | | | | | |
| 2. Feel most outgoing | | | | | | | | | | | | |
| Feel most withdrawn | | | | | | | | | | | | |
| 3. Eat least | | | | | | | | | | | | |
| Eat most | | | | | | | | | | | | |
| 4. Lose most weight | | | | | | | | | | | | |
| Gain most weight | | | | | | | | | | | | |
| 5. Sleep the least | | | | | | | | | | | | |
| Sleep the most | | | | | | | | | | | | |
| 6. Feel energetic | | | | | | | | | | | | |
| Feel fatigued | | | | | | | | | | | | |
| 7. Gain interest in sex | | | | | | | | | | | | |
| Lose interest in sex | | | | | | | | | | | | |

compelled to have an answer for every category. For example, you might be able to identify one or more months during the year when you usually feel exceptionally hungry and no months at all when your appetite falls below its normal level.

Now, for each of the seven categories, take a pencil and, beginning with January, draw a continuous line from one marked square to the next marked square, curving the line up or down as required. For instance, in category 5, if you slept most in January, February,

March, November and December and least in June and July, draw a line through the first three months and continue it up at an angle to take in June and July, then angle it back down to catch November and December.

5. Sleep the least

   Sleep the most

Notice the continuous curve. The lines you draw might not look exactly like this one. They may have more peaks and troughs, or none at all; some people only experience a change in one direction. As mentioned

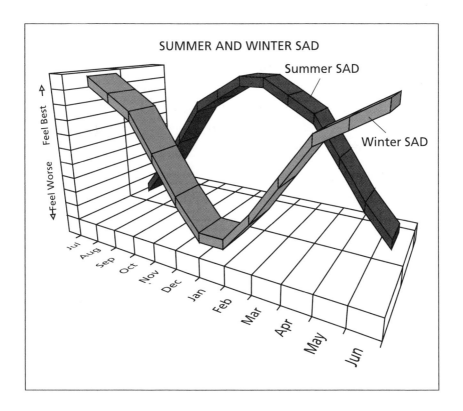

SUMMER AND WINTER SAD

Summer SAD

Winter SAD

Feel Best

Feel Worse

Jul Aug Sep Oct Nov Dec Jan Feb Mar Apr May Jun

earlier, perhaps your appetite increases at a certain time of the year but at other times of the year never drops below your normal level.

The important thing to look for is *similarities* in seasonal occurrence between one category and the next. Do you have a number of curves that peak or bottom out during the same season? If you see a decided trend toward troughs in fall or winter, you likely have the winter form of seasonal affective disorder. On the other hand, if curves for categories 1, 2, 6 and 7 bottom out in spring or summer, you are a candidate for the summer form of SAD. And, although the condition is very rare, if you have dips in your curves at both times of year, you could have both summer and winter SAD — or neither. The more often depression settles in over the course of the year, the more difficult it is to confirm its seasonal nature. SAD is only one of several mood disorders. Unless the seasonal pattern of your depressive episodes is quite distinct, your doctor might not diagnose you as having SAD.

# SAD Self-Assessment

## Section 2: Your Degree of SADness

Consider, as the seasons change, how greatly each of the following factors change. Assign a numerical value to your answers: 0 = no noticeable change, 1 = only a slight change, 2 = moderate change, 3 = very noticeable change, 4 = extremely noticeable change.

| | |
|---|---|
| Your sense of well-being: | _____ |
| The amount you socialize: | _____ |
| Your appetite: | _____ |
| Your weight*: | _____ |
| How much you sleep: | _____ |
| Your energy level: | _____ |
| Total | _____ |

*Use the following as a guideline:
 1-3 lbs. = 1; 4-7 lbs. = 2; 8-11 lbs. = 3; 12+ lbs. = 4.

The total score you have just come up with will help determine if you are clinically SAD, seasonally blue or relatively unaffected by this syndrome.

Your score should total no more than 24. If it comes to 7 or less, you are within normal bounds. **Everyone sees some degree of annual fluctuation in their mood or eating and sleeping habits.**

If your score falls between 8 and 11, you notice decided changes in your mood and behavior as the seasons come and go. These changes, although annoying, do not seriously interfere with your ability to cope either at work or in your personal relationships. You have the seasonal blues and will likely benefit considerably by following the self-help tips outlined later in this book.

What about those of you who scored 12 and up? Yes, you may be suffering a clinical dose of seasonal affective disorder. If your score is in the upper part of the range and your symptoms are seriously getting in the way of leading a normal, productive life, visit your family physician. This is critical in getting an accurate assessment. Although the lifestyle suggestions and light therapy described later in this book can help you immensely, you might find it difficult to use them if you are in the grip of a deep episode of depression. Your family doctor can confirm that you do indeed have SAD and take immediate measures to get you back on an even keel. **A confirmation of diagnosis is extremely important.** As you will see farther along in this book,

## Case Study: JEAN

Jean, now 50, has had seasonal affective disorder for 20 years. She says her symptoms varied in severity from winter to winter until seven years ago, when they got so bad she simply "stopped functioning."

Her husband finally had to go with Jean to their family doctor to back up her complaints, which had gone totally unheeded to that point. "I was put on Prozac, which made me *too* calm," says Jean. "So we looked for alternatives and decided to try light therapy. It worked within weeks. I felt like saying 'YEAH!' **It's just like summer every day during light treatment.**"

there are a number of other syndromes and disorders that display symptoms similar to those experienced in SAD but which require considerably different courses of treatment. As well, you will need to be under a doctor's supervision to self-administer or receive light therapy.

## Finding a SAD Doctor

Discuss SAD with your family doctor as a first step toward obtaining the right diagnosis and treatment. One advantage of this approach is that your doctor most likely has seen you in your non-SAD state over a period of several years. Your SADness should be reasonably obvious by comparison. If your doctor diagnoses SAD, or suspects you are suffering from the syndrome, you might be referred to a specialist.

Some people find their family doctor is either unknowledgeable about SAD or is reluctant to acknowledge it exists. Seasonal affective disorder only recently obtained status as a bona fide medical problem (in 1984). It takes time for news of this nature to spread throughout the medical community and gain general acceptance.

But you need help NOW. **Finding a doctor who knows what seasonal affective disorder is — and how to treat it — is critical.** If a trip to your family doctor proves unfruitful, consult the lists of SAD researchers, light therapy clinics and mood disorder support groups provided in Appendices C and D for a person or organization that can refer you to a knowledgeable doctor reasonably close to where you live.

X

The cutoff point between the seasonal blues and clinical SAD is by no means an exact line. In this type of assessment there is always a bit of give and take. If your score is on the borderline between the seasonal blues and clinical SAD, you can fine-tune your self-assessment by answering the following questions:

1. Has anyone in your immediate family (father, mother, sister, brother, uncle, aunt or grandparent) been diagnosed with or shown signs of having seasonal affective disorder or any other mood disorder?

2. Has there been any history of alcoholism in your immediate family?

3. Do you notice a dramatic change in your mood or behavior, either for the better or worse, when you travel to a different climate? Do you return to your original condition when you come home (assuming you return within the same season you departed)?

4. Have you required help from your family doctor to deal with depression, oversleeping, increased appetite, fatigue or lack of interest in sex?

A positive answer to any one of these four questions **may** indicate you have clinical SAD. But check with your doctor. If none of the above situations apply to you, you more likely have the seasonal blues.

(From Rosenthal, Bradt and Wehr's *Seasonal Pattern Assessment Questionnaire*, National Institute of Mental Health, Bethesda, Maryland, 1984. Adapted by permission.)

# Welcome to the Club!

If you are SAD or blue, you are not alone, especially if you suffer in the wintertime and live in the northern United States or Canada. The winter form of SAD (there is also a summer SAD) is most common and the number of people affected by seasonal affective disorder during the winter months increases the farther north you live. Several studies have been carried out in the United States and Canada to get a handle on the exact number

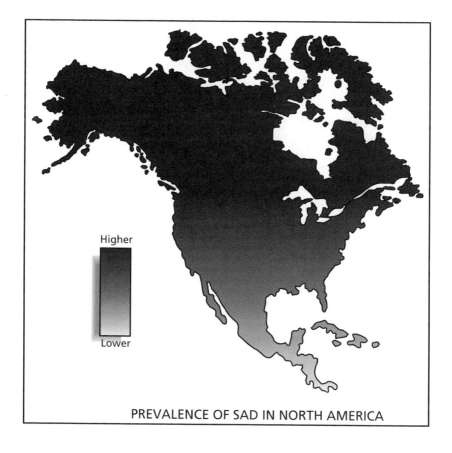

Higher

Lower

PREVALENCE OF SAD IN NORTH AMERICA

of people involved. It is estimated that only 1.4 percent of people in Florida suffer full-blown winter SAD, whereas 10.2 percent of residents in close proximity to either side of the U.S.-Canada border are severely affected.

If this last statistic seems high; if you live in these geographic locations but still can't identify one out of every ten people you know as suffering from severe SAD, you could be right. This figure is controversial. One survey of New York City residents shows 4.7 percent have full-blown SAD. Dr. Raymond Lam, a Vancouver-based SAD researcher, puts the incidence of clinical SAD in Canada at two to three percent of the population. That still represents 500,000 to 750,000 Canadians (based on a population of 25 million)!

Add to these figures the vast number of people who are not clinically SAD but still labor every winter under the milder effects of the seasonal blues. The generally accepted estimate of winter blues sufferers is 10 to 15 percent of the population. The total number of winter "SAD" plus "blue" people jumps up to somewhere between 12 and 25 percent in the northern United States and Canada.

In the next chapter we will define SAD, identify its symptoms and look at several more real-life cases. Try to pick out any symptoms or situations that feel familiar, as this will help you understand your own condition and its level of severity.

# CHAPTER 2

# What Is SAD?

**S**AD IS AN APT ACRONYM FOR A SYN-
drome, or cluster of symptoms, called "seasonal
affective disorder." In psychiatric lingo, "affective" means mood, so an affective disorder is one in
which your mood is abnormally high or low. What
makes SAD unique from other mood disorders is the
fact that your abnormal mood episodes occur at the
same time of year on a regular basis.

Many observant scholars over the course of history
have remarked on certain aspects of human health, both
physical and mental, that suggest some connection with
the seasons. And we have all heard the odd bit of folk
wisdom or old wives' tale that ties an ache here, a mel-
ancholia there, to a particular season. But the underlying concept of seasonal affective disorder — the idea
that many people can and do experience aberrations in
mood, appetite, energy levels, sleep patterns and sex
drive on a recurring seasonal basis — has only gained
widespread acceptance during the past decade.

The self-assessment you completed in the first chapter is based on the Seasonal Pattern Assessment Questionnaire developed by Dr. Norman Rosenthal and his
colleagues at the National Institute of Mental Health
in Bethesda, Maryland. They were among the first to
recognize the *interrelated* nature of the symptoms of
SAD. In 1984, Dr. Rosenthal and his group published

the results of breakthrough research that established seasonal affective disorder as a real medical condition with distinct symptoms. They even came up with an effective course of treatment — light therapy. From that point doctors have been able to both diagnose the disorder with some confidence and alleviate their patients' symptoms. There is hope!

# Officially Speaking

The *Diagnostic and Statistical Manual of Mental Disorders* — the authoritative reference work used by psychiatrists (see "Further Reading") — recognizes seasonal affective disorder as a subtype of *major depression*. If there is no organic cause or emotional upset such as the recent loss of a loved one, you would likely (but not necessarily) be diagnosed as suffering a major depression if, over the course of a two-week period, for most of nearly every day you exhibited (1) a depressed mood or (2) a markedly diminished interest or pleasure in all, or almost all, activities, and also displayed at least four of the following symptoms:

- A loss or gain of more than five percent of body weight in a month (assuming you were not on a diet) or a consistent increase or decrease in appetite
- Either inability to sleep or oversleeping nearly every day
- A near daily feeling of agitation or, conversely, a feeling of slowing down
- Fatigue or loss of energy
- Inappropriate or excessive feelings of guilt or worthlessness

- Inability to think or concentrate at normal capacity, or indecisiveness
- Recurrent bouts of death thoughts or an attempt at suicide

As well, to qualify as a major depressive episode, the above symptoms would have to be severe enough to cause you considerable distress or impair your ability to function normally in social situations and at work.

Now for the SAD part. The same manual lists four more criteria that must be met in order to come up with a diagnosis of seasonal affective disorder:

- Your episode(s) of major depression must begin during a specific season of the year on a regular basis. For example, your depression might begin like clockwork nearly every winter.
- The symptoms of your depressive episode(s) must disappear of their own accord during a specific season on a regular basis. For many SAD sufferers spring is the season they look forward to.
- Over the past two years you have experienced two of these seasonal episodes with no depressive episodes showing up out of season.
- During the course of your lifetime, the number of seasonal episodes of depression you have experienced far outnumber any episodes that might have taken place out of season.

# What's Going on Here?

We still do not know exactly what goes wrong in the human body to bring about seasonal affective disorder. Since 1984, a large number of inquisitive researchers around the world have solved parts of the puzzle, but there are still many pieces missing.

As creatures of the earth, our bodies have evolved to cope with the annual changes in our environment. Most people handle the seasonal swings in temperature, humidity, number of daylight hours and the like,

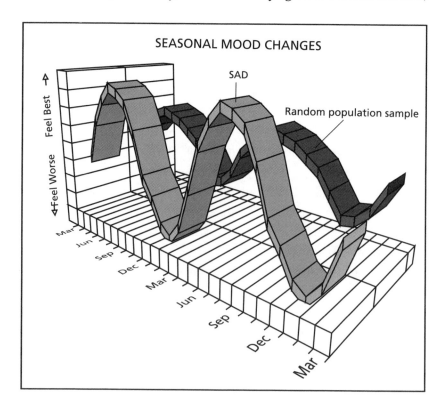

SEASONAL MOOD CHANGES

just fine. Others don't. Something has gone wrong that prevents the normal functioning of their built-in seasonal regulators.

We know that the winter form of seasonal affective disorder is a dysfunction of the human body that appears to be related to a lack of sufficient exposure to light. Seasons work their way into the picture by way of the decreased amount of natural sunlight during the winter months. Since, in the northern hemisphere, the closer you live to the North Pole the less sunshine you get over the winter, it follows that residents of the northern United States and Canada are living in two of the most SAD-prone places on earth.

# It's Normal to be a Bit SAD from Time to Time

It is estimated that as many as one out of every four people suffers the symptoms of seasonal affective disorder to some degree. This ranges from mild symptoms that make the daily grind a bit more difficult, the seasonal blues, to full-blown clinical SAD.

Sleep patterns and weight changes, even among non-SAD people, follow the seasons in the same way as winter SAD. The changes are simply not as pronounced. What is normal? Most people sleep more in winter and less in summer, in harmony with the hours

**A Closer Look at Seasonal Trends**

Most people experience regular changes in mood, sociability, sleep and weight that parallel the annual changes SAD people go through. The difference is in the degree these factors fluctuate. People with SAD find the changes to be much more pronounced.

### SEASONAL SLEEP TRENDS
▬■▬ SAD
▬●▬ Random population sample

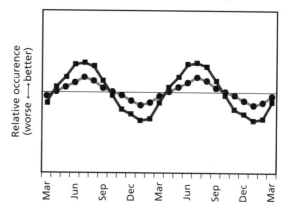

### SEASONAL WEIGHT TRENDS
▬■▬ SAD
▬●▬ Random population sample

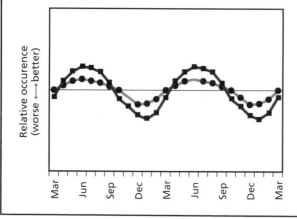

These four graphs compare the changes experienced by clinically SAD people with those experienced by a random sampling of the population. The graphs are adapted from data collected by Dr. Michael Terman of the New York State Psychiatric Institute and used here with his permission.

### SEASONAL MOOD TRENDS
- SAD
- Random population sample

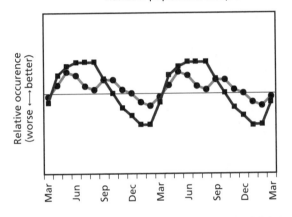

### SEASONAL SOCIAL ACTIVITY TRENDS
- SAD
- Random population sample

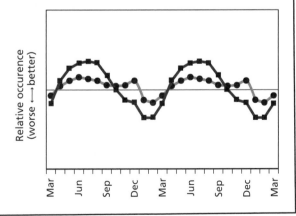

25

of sunlight and timing of the dawn. Likewise, it is common to prefer "heavier," more substantial meals on cold winter days and light fare in the heat of summer. In seasonally blue and SAD people, these changes in lifestyle are more severe and are accompanied by a number of other symptoms.

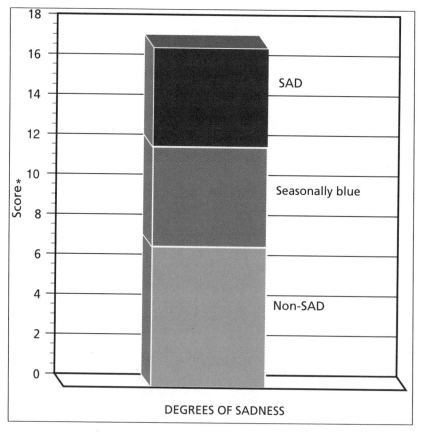

*See your assessment score on page 13.

# CHAPTER 3

# Symptoms of SAD

SEASONAL AFFECTIVE DISORDER IS A specific type of depressive mood disorder. But if you compare the symptoms of SAD to those of typical depression, you might be surprised.

Besides low mood, the symptoms of depression include insomnia, lack of appetite, weight loss, lack of libido, and fatigue. Fifteen to 30 percent of clinically SAD people display these classic symptoms of depression. Yet most SAD people complain of symptoms that are completely different from the typical symptoms. For example, instead of having insomnia, many SAD sufferers find it difficult to stay awake. Classically depressed individuals lose their appetites; an all too voracious appetite in SAD people leads to weight gain rather than loss. On the other hand, fatigue and little or no interest in sex are symptoms common to both classic depression and SAD.

Not all SAD sufferers experience atypical symptoms of depression. True, most SAD people do but there is a commonality between sufferers with the typical set of symptoms and those with atypical ones. It might even be possible to switch from one set of symptoms to the other. Although it has not been described in the psychiatric literature, Dr. Chris Gorman, a SAD researcher, says it is his impression from examining many SAD patients that moderately SAD individuals usually complain of suffering atypical symptoms and, if they later become more severely depressed, they complain of having the standard symptoms.

How long does seasonal affective disorder usually afflict a person? In a highly comprehensive study carried out in a clinic in Italy (which is at the same latitude as the National Institute of Mental Health in Bethesda, Maryland, a hotbed of SAD research activity), Gianni Faedda and his colleagues found that most of their patients experienced the symptoms of SAD over a period of nearly 12 years. Interestingly, though, these symptoms did not beset them every year, but rather, on average, 70 percent of the time, or seven years out of ten.

Let's have a closer look at the common symptoms associated with seasonal affective disorder.

# Depression

If you have winter SAD, "fall" is a highly appropriate name for the time of year when your spirits begin to drop as suddenly as the leaves off the trees. The dark days of winter are imminent. You feel a profound sense of hopelessness descend over your world. Thanksgiving arrives and you grumble to yourself there is precious little to be thankful for. And the joy of Christmas — what's that? Who cares! You withdraw from your friends and family more and more, shunning parties and even the obligatory family get-togethers. People begin to notice your absence and, with every well-meaning inquiry, you sink further into your shell, feeling guilty you can't muster what it takes to be a good parent, a loving spouse, a productive employee, an understanding friend. You obsess for hours on what a thoroughly inadequate excuse for a human being you must be. Your self-esteem plummets. And the days just keep getting shorter.

*Hopelessness, an inability to experience joy, apathy, guilt, sadness, decreased talkativeness, confusion, forgetfulness, withdrawal* and *lack of self-esteem* are all aspects of depression encountered by people with seasonal affective disorder. In their most severe forms, these thoughts and feelings can be devastating. They can ruin marriages

and friendships. They can destroy careers. And they can lead to thoughts of suicide.

Fortunately, thinking about suicide is not as common among those with SAD as it is among people with non-seasonal mood disorders. In addition, although someone with SAD might think about committing suicide, it is rare for a SAD individual to actually attempt it.

Another aspect of depression that differs between people with non-seasonal mood disorders and people with SAD is the **time of day** when they feel most down. More often than not, those who suffer non-seasonal depression are at their worst in the morning. The majority of SAD people are most despondent and impaired in the afternoon and evening.

All the above mood impairments can show up in various combinations and degrees of severity. If you are seasonally blue, you might have the odd day when your spirits are low enough to bring on an urge to withdraw from the world but, unless you can afford that luxury, you don't. You grudgingly go to work or very quietly and unenthusiastically fulfill a social commitment. You get by. And although your life might seem terribly uninteresting or somehow not worthwhile, you don't consider ending it.

How long do these bouts of depression last? If you are seasonally blue they can be extremely fleeting, lasting a few hours, a day, maybe an entire week. If you are clinically SAD, your depression is a constant companion for two weeks at the least. You might experience several episodes of depression over the winter or you might go into depression in the fall and not emerge until spring. The average length of depressive episode found in one study was five months.

You may find there are years when you don't succumb to depression at all. The symptoms of seasonal affective disorder do not necessarily show up every

## Case Study: BARBARA

Barbara was despondent. At 48 years of age she was no closer to finding a cure for her annual winter depression and arthralgia than when the symptoms first showed up in her teenage years. Over the years, Barbara had consulted many psychiatrists and was hospitalized briefly for depression at one point. Tricyclic antidepressants were a write-off; the side effects proved to be too severe for her to tolerate. Eventually she was diagnosed as having chronic fatigue syndrome, in spite of the fact her Epstein-Barr virus test came back negative.

Nonetheless, all the signs of SAD were there. Like clockwork, every November her mood and energy levels dropped, she withdrew from her usual social commitments, lost interest in sex, slept a lot, gained as much as 20 pounds during the winter from overeating, thought about committing suicide now and again, and experienced feelings of guilt and anxiety. Then right on cue, all these symptoms would disappear in April. There was a history of mood disorders within her family; Barbara's sister had committed suicide by jumping off a bridge. Once the SAD nature of her ailment was recognized, two weeks of light therapy successfully banished her symptoms and significantly reduced her arthralgia.

*— based on Dr. Raymond Lam's clinical research*

year. You fit the most common SAD profile if you run into episodes of depression an average of seven years out of ten.

You can actually feel depression creeping up on you in any situation that deprives you of light: the short, gloomy days of winter, a household or office with too little natural or artificial light, a run of cloudy weather — even during spring or summer. On the other hand, clear, sunny days in mid-winter can lead to some relief from your symptoms (assuming it is warm enough and your lifestyle allows you to get outdoors).

## Rating Your Depression

How badly you are affected by depression can vary with many factors — the seasons, the weather, your household or office "built" environment and the effectiveness of the treatment you are receiving.

**How can you judge the severity of your depression and get an accurate reading on whether or not your condition is improving with light therapy, medication and/or lifestyle change?**

Professionals use standard tools for measuring depression. The Hamilton Depression Rating Scale (HDRS) is one. While it is not the only assessment tool at their disposal, in the case of SAD, it is used more often than others. Dr. Janet B. W. Williams and her colleagues at the New York State Psychiatric Institute have worked out a specialized form of this assessment device that takes into account the atypical depressive symptoms of SAD. Without this modification, many SAD people would not test out as being seriously depressed! This is because they exhibit exactly the opposite symptoms to those seen in non-seasonal depression, the form of depression for which the HDRS was originally designed.

This type of assessment has two strengths when it comes to researching the beneficial effects of light therapy and medication on SAD individuals. First, if everyone is assessed using the same set of criteria, it is easier to compare the results of vastly different studies. For instance, can 30 minutes per day of light therapy lift your depression as effectively as a prescription for Prozac? Second, your degree of depression is assessed by a trained clinician. The clinician is objective in a way that patient self-assessments cannot be.

# Oversleeping

It is quite normal to feel like sleeping in a little later on those dark, cold mornings of winter. You think to yourself, *The sun's not up yet. Why should I be?* At an unconscious level, your sleep regulator in the brain is responding in much the same way. It has evolved over the eons to set your internal wake-up call to an hour appropriate for the time of year. In the winter you naturally sleep in a bit later, and in the summer you may get out of bed at an hour that leaves you wondering what in the world you are going to do to fill all the time before noon.

It might not be valid in today's urban, comfortable bedrooms, but at one time there was considerable survival value in regulating hours of sleep by the season. Over the course of human history, there was little point in waking up before dawn. In the winter months, being up before the sun meant wasting precious reserves of energy scrambling around in the dark, trying to get anything accomplished in the coldest hours of the day. It was much better to remain asleep, at a lower metabolic rate, until the light and warmth of the sun's rays were available. In the summertime, it was better to wake up with the sun at an early hour because you did not want to be caught unawares by some beast on the prowl for breakfast.

If you are afflicted by the winter blues or a more severe form of SAD, your sleep regulator has somehow gone awry in its judgement of just how much sleep you really require. Sleeping in well past noon is not uncommon. Approximately four out of every five SAD individuals who experience sleep problems report sleeping

## Case Study: RANDY

Every winter Randy felt like hibernating. "I'd make it to work, but as soon as I got home, I'd go straight to bed," says Randy. "I just didn't have any energy. **I'd sleep from 8 p.m. until 6 a.m. and still not feel like I'd had any sleep.**"

Now Randy benefits from 30 minutes of light therapy every morning, from late September through March or April. He claims, "It's been so successful that I also use light treatment at other times of the year when the weather turns rainy for a week or more."

in several hours longer during the dark months of fall and winter. And a similar percentage find it difficult to stay awake during the day, experiencing considerable drowsiness and a tendency to nap. This increase in the amount you sleep is called *hypersomnia*.

Some SAD people suffer *insomnia* (the typical sleep dysfunction seen with depression) rather than *oversleeping* (an atypical symptom). These insomniacs find it impossible to rack up many hours of sleep at night. Still others find the number of hours they sleep has not changed; however, these hours have shifted on the clock. For instance, they find it extremely difficult to fall asleep until quite late, then they don't wake up until a correspondingly late hour in the morning.

Regardless of whether you are sleeping too much or too little, once awake, it is doubtful you are in a good mood and anticipating a cheery, bright day ahead.

## Case Study: EMMA

"I began attending the local light therapy clinic three years ago because I was sleeping constantly most of the winter — not an easy thing to do with kids," chuckles Emma. "I didn't have serious depression, but I was very withdrawn due to fatigue. Light therapy made winter seem like summer. Now that I have my lights, I'm even enjoying Christmases for the first time in my life."

# Fatigue

It is difficult to get out of bed in the morning, maybe impossible. If you do make it to your feet, throw on the least crumpled and worn outfit you can dig up without too much effort and get off to work, you tire early in the day. More likely than not, you simply call in sick. There just isn't another drop of energy left to get any further than the nearest couch or bed. What is wrong?

What seems to be the underlying issue in the case of the hypersomnia experienced by most SAD people is the quantity of sleep they are getting vs. the quality of sleep. Research carried out at the National Institute of Mental Health has demonstrated that SAD people sleep more but, in the long run, get fewer hours of quality sleep than non-SAD people. During the night, it is not at all unusual to awaken several times. Studies also have shown that hypersomnic SAD individuals get less delta sleep during the winter. This is the type of deep sleep that normally leaves you feeling well-rested and energetic upon rising in the morning.

In other words, as contradictory as it might sound, even though you may be sleeping an extra amount, it is highly probable you are suffering from the effects of sleep deprivation!

Try to imagine the impression SAD can make on your friends, family and colleagues.

## Case Study: ELLEN

Ellen is a part-time instructor at a major Canadian university. One winter term she had a student enrolled in her class who was obviously suffering from some sort of disabling, degenerative disease; as the term progressed, this student grew pale and fatigued, found it increasingly difficult to maintain her grades and eventually gave up on her personal appearance. Ellen knew this young woman kept pet birds and worried to herself that her student might have contracted parrot disease.

Class ended in early April and several weeks later Ellen was approached one day by a healthy, well-groomed young lady she didn't recognize. It turned out to be the same student, who assured Ellen she hadn't been dying of an exotic disease earlier in the year, but did suffer badly from seasonal affective disorder.

# Overeating

So you thought it was simply the overabundance of sweets and other tasty food during the holiday season that added those pounds? There may be more to the story if you have seasonal affective disorder.

Appetite regulation is a major problem for many people with SAD. Studies carried out in the United States, Canada and Great Britain show up to 84 percent of SAD patients crave carbohydrates and sweets during the winter months, while up to 76 percent notice a marked increase in appetite.

Why? Don't large portions of pasta, potatoes, rice and beans usually lead to a profound sense of drowsiness and an urge to nap after mealtime? Isn't this exactly the type of diet someone with SAD, already predisposed to fatigue and oversleeping, would instinctively avoid like the plague?

Well, as it turns out, instinct does have something to do with appetite. High-carbohydrate meals energize SAD people! The same meals that usually slow down non-SAD people have the opposite effect on people with seasonal affective disorder. Ooey-gooey sweets, mashed potatoes and thick stews are only a few of the "comfort foods" SAD people instinctively turn to in order to boost serotonin levels in the brain. Serotonin is an important chemical that transmits messages of well-being and calm. In non-SAD people, it can bring on a state of sleepiness. But serotonin doesn't seem to have the same effect on SAD individuals, probably because they are starting with a lower level of serotonin. Studies have shown that, when administered tryptophan (a precursor of serotonin), SAD people become positively euphoric instead of slowed down. Serotonin acts as a naturally occurring antidepressant for SAD victims. By eating foods that lead to the generation of serotonin, SAD people are instinctively self-treating their depression with a quick pick-me-up.

There is one unhappy consequence of this boon. In this subconscious attempt to fight off depression, people with seasonal affective disorder often lose sight of the overall amount of food they are taking in on a daily basis. The greatest part of their increased nutrient intake usually comes in the form of carbohydrates, while consumption of foods high in protein and fat remains the same.

**Case Study: JOHN**

John, a 35-year-old SAD sufferer from Nova Scotia, writes: "My ice cream and carbohydrate craving is much harder to control than my craving for alcohol was when I first gave up drinking. **I can honestly tell you that I can sit down and eat a whole 4-liter container of Butterscotch Ripple ice cream in one sitting.** I'm not satisfied until I clean the container out. Sometimes my stomach feels like it will burst, but I just can't control myself. In a 7-day week, I can usually eat 4 liters on 3 days, and 2 liters on 3 days. I try to go one day out of 7 without any ice cream at all, just to try and show myself that I have some control over my life. But let me tell you, getting through that one day without a taste of ice cream is a nerve-testing, hard old day."

Not surprisingly, weight gains over the winter ranging from 12 to 20 pounds and more are not unusual. It is also not unusual to see many, if not all, of these pounds drop off in the spring when SAD people finally begin feeling themselves again, stop binging on fattening foods and get outside for some fresh air and exercise. Wonderful as it may be to shed these pounds, the resulting cyclical, seasonal weight gain and loss can prove a bit rough on your clothing situation. Many SAD patients have a "yo-yo" wardrobe that goes up and down the size chart to accommodate their annual swings in girth.

The really good news is that SAD individuals who find overeating to be a major problem are particularly responsive to light therapy. **Studies have shown that light therapy can fully reverse the symptoms of increased appetite and carbohydrate craving.**

# Lack of Sex Drive

You have been lying in bed for the last hour, half awake, watching the 10 o'clock news with its usual lineup of murders, bombings and natural disasters. As a result,

you are feeling even more depressed, irritable and at odds with the world than you were before. You are enormously tired. Sleep seems the logical way to escape the day's disappointments. And now your partner wants to do *what*?

People with seasonal affective disorder display a decided disinterest in sex during the months of fall and winter. In fact, if you look at the birth dates of the children of SAD individuals and, from there, work backward to the probable dates of conception of these children, you see a definite grouping of conception dates in the spring and summer months as opposed to the fall and winter months. So, although it may be difficult for your partner to understand that your lack of interest in sex is a side effect of SAD and nothing personal, the up side of the situation is that this symptom, like the others, passes as spring rolls around. Some people with seasonal affective disorder even become highly interested in sex in the spring (much to their partner's delight). But do beware. Sometimes this increase in libido can exceed the bounds of good judgement, as we shall see in the section on "spring mania" in Chapter 4.

# Winter SAD vs. Summer SAD

As research progresses, it is becoming clear that a summer form of seasonal affective disorder exists and sufferers of summer SAD are not quite as rare as first believed. Researchers at SAD clinics around the world are reporting anywhere from about 12 percent to 50 percent of their patients have the summer form of seasonal affective disorder.

Unlike winter SAD, there appears to be no correlation between latitude and summer SAD. This is not surprising. Summer SAD sufferers tend to identify heat and humidity as the environmental triggers that bring about their symptoms, more often than lack of sufficient sunlight.

Light treatment does not seem to be effective against summer SAD. Rather, in cases where heat and humidity appear to be at the root of summer SAD, a combination of exposure to cold and isolation from heat has proven to alleviate the symptoms. In one experiment carried out by Wehr et al., a patient who had suffered from summer SAD for 15 years was confined to an air-conditioned house for five days. During this period she took several 15-minute-long cold showers every day.

By the fifth day she had improved dramatically, but relapse occurred nine days after her treatment stopped.

Another proven antidote is travel to a less hot and humid climate. Researchers in the Washington, D.C., area — a truly muggy place to live — have noticed that local residents severely afflicted with summer SAD are no longer prone to the disorder when they spend the summer in New England. But, as they say, everything is relative. One person, who grew up in the extreme north of Canada, has come forth to say that she finds the moderate climate of summer in Calgary oppressively hot and, as a result, she regularly suffers the summer blues.

The demographic profile of the typical summer SAD person also varies somewhat from that of the winter SAD person. In general, summer SAD seems to afflict an older segment of the population. Whereas winter SAD is common among those as young as 20 years of age, summer SAD tends to be more prevalent among those who are over 30. Men also seem to be more prone to summer SAD than to winter SAD.

For most of these people, summer depressive episodes begin in April, but many also report onset in March and May. Overall, studies have established there is a much larger degree of variation in onset time for summer SAD than for winter SAD. Whereas most winter SAD episodes of depression begin in September — give or take a little more than half a month either way — the onset of summer SAD depression can vary by more than a month on either side of April, the peak month. Summer SAD also differs from winter SAD in its length of duration. In one study, winter SAD depression was shown to last an average of 5.6 months versus 4.8 months for summer SAD.

# Symptoms of Summer SAD

In contrast to those rebellious symptoms of winter SAD that refuse to fall in line with the standard attributes of depressive disorders, the symptoms of summer seasonal affective disorder are far more conventional. The line-up of summer symptoms includes *depression, agitation, insomnia, loss of appetite, lack of energy* and *nominal sex drive.*

A number of these symptoms doubtless sound familiar. The lack of energy and sex drive are common to both summer SAD and winter SAD. So, too, is the depression, the loss of interest and pleasure in life, sadness, hopelessness, guilt, decreased talkativeness, low self-esteem and withdrawal from family and friends — these symptoms all show up in the summer months.

Those who experience the depression of summer SAD have an unfortunate factor working against them. The amount of serotonin, the chemical messenger in the brain that exudes feelings of well-being, fluctuates over the course of the year and is at its lowest level in spring and early summer. The double whammy of SAD plus the underabundance of serotonin is very likely behind the statistics that show summer SAD individuals think about suicide more often than people with winter SAD.

*A note to friends and family of SAD sufferers: No mention of suicidal thoughts should go unheeded. If someone confides in you that they have been considering taking their own life, strongly encourage that person to seek out professional help — immediately.*

Commonly experienced symptoms of summer SAD that run counter to those of winter SAD are *agitation*, *insomnia* and *lack of appetite*. Although fatigued, there is an inability to settle down. Instead of sleeping an inordinate part of the day away, many summer SAD sufferers report an inability to get enough sleep to function at an alert level the next day. Oversleeping is not unheard of, however.

Lack of appetite is perhaps the most strikingly different aspect of summer SAD. The binging on carbohydrate-laden foods and sweets common in winter SAD is rarely encountered. This lack of interest in food, and the resultant loss of weight, is fully in line with the behavioral pattern found in non-seasonal depression.

Too little sleep. Inadequate nutrition. It's no mystery why you are feeling SO TIRED.

# Suffering from Winter and Summer SAD?

Yes, it is possible to experience both the winter and summer forms of seasonal affective disorder! A precious few months in spring and fall are the only respite from symptoms, then it's back into the depths of depression again. The number of people in this unfortunate position is rather small. One study carried out in New York City by Dr. Michael Terman and his colleagues found that people who fell into the winter SAD category outnumbered those who suffered SAD in both winter and summer by 7.5 to 1.

Another variation on this theme is winter and summer depression with spring and fall mania. An incredible mental roller coaster ride! Dr. Thomas Wehr of the National Institute of Mental Health reports that one of his SAD patients experienced depression from June to August and from December to January every year, and swung to the opposite extreme in the months between.

# Get a Professional Diagnosis

At this point you probably have formed an opinion about your susceptibility to seasonal affective disorder, based on the self-assessment you completed at the beginning of this book and by comparing your own condition to the case studies presented along the way. If you suspect you fall into the category of full-blown SAD, it would be wise to consult your family physician to obtain a definite diagnosis. Many of the symptoms associated with SAD are symptomatic of other disorders that require an entirely different course of treatment. Here are some of the most common candidates for a mix up:

## • Underactive thyroid gland

An intolerance of cold weather, an overall loss of your get up and go, and weight gain resulting from lethargy are prime markers of this condition, which goes by the medical name *hypothyroidism*. You can see how the aversion to winter, fatigue and weight problem could easily be attributed to seasonal affective disorder at first glance. Dr. Russell Joffe's work in Toronto at the Clarke Institute of Psychiatry has shown a close relationship between mood disorders, in general, and the functioning of the thyroid gland. A separate, preliminary study carried out by Dr. A.M. Ghadirian at McGill University has found hypothyroidism more common among SAD patients than patients with other mood disorders.

Your thyroid gland (located near the voice box in your throat) is the source of a hormone that determines how fast your body burns up, or metabolizes, the food you ingest. When your thyroid fails to come up with enough of this hormone, as is the case in hypothyroidism, your metabolism slows down. The amount of energy normally supplied to your muscles through the metabolic process drops and you burn off a smaller percentage of the calories you eat, resulting in weight gain.

Treatment for hypothyroidism is quite different from the treatment for SAD. Light therapy won't work but supplementation of the thyroid hormone in pill form has proven to be most effective.

### • Low blood sugar

Both seasonal affective disorder and low blood sugar (*hypoglycemia*) have these symptoms: fatigue, irritability, headaches, increased appetite, and a craving for sweets. But people with low blood sugar usually experience fatigue and a sense of light-headedness an hour or two after meals, the time when most SAD people are feeling energized. There is also no seasonality to hypoglycemia.

This is not a condition to be taken lightly. Hypoglycemia is brought about by too much insulin in your system. Eating sugary foods only increases the amount of insulin, which, paradoxically, further lowers the level of sugar in your blood. Because blood sugar plays an essential role in the proper functioning of your brain, dangerously low levels can result in severe mental dysfunction, coma and even death.

A simple blood test can reveal if you are hypoglycemic and the condition can then be kept under control through diet. Eating several small meals over the day, rather than a few large meals, paces out the absorption of sugar into your bloodstream. Avoid simple carbohydrates (sugary sweets) that are absorbed too readily into your system. Concentrate on foods high in **complex carbohydrates** and **proteins** that take longer to be absorbed and used by your body.

## • **Bulimia nervosa**

This exotic-sounding eating disorder refers to severe, uncontrollable carbohydrate cravings that can result in obesity. Researchers have recently discovered that the behavioral patterns and attitudes regarding food and self-image associated with *bulimia nervosa* are the same as seen in many people suffering from SAD. In fact, a large percentage of people with SAD not only exhibit the same symptoms, but experience them to the same degree.

Increased appetite, weight gain and dysfunctional eating attitudes form the common ground between bulimia nervosa and SAD. There is also a seasonality to bulimia nervosa. Individuals with this disorder tend to binge on high-carbohydrate foods slightly less over the summer months. Researchers are beginning to

## Case Study: MOLLY

For five long years, Molly struggled in the grips of bulimia nervosa. Every day she went through a routine in which she stuffed down large amounts of food then induced vomiting, sometimes as many as three times in one 24-hour period. Molly needed help and was hospitalized on several occasions. The drug fenfluramine decreased the frequency of her binging episodes, but other antidepressants did nothing for her. Then someone noticed that Molly fit the SAD profile in winter and, although her binging episodes continued year round, they were less frequent in the summer. Could light therapy help? Yes! After two weeks of treatment Molly's depression lifted and the frequency of her binging dropped dramatically.

— *based on Dr. Raymond Lam's clinical research*

suspect there is a significant connection between the two disorders. They might have a common underlying cause or, as in the case of chronic fatigue syndrome, there may be a considerable number of misdiagnosed bulimia nervosa patients who actually have SAD. Dr. Lam in Vancouver has successfully treated a bulimic woman using light therapy. The question is whether the light therapy was effective because the two disorders are caused by the same biological mechanism, or did the patient have SAD underlying her bulimia? Further research should tell the tale.

## • Chronic Fatigue Syndrome

Every fall we gear up for another flu season. The elderly and people with ailing immune systems roll up their sleeves to be inoculated with the latest strain of flu vaccine while other people duck sneezes in elevators and wash their hands (with warm water and soap) more often. When the flu does strike, you feel miserable and incredibly tired for a couple of weeks and then gradually regain your strength as your health returns — unless you have chronic fatigue syndrome.

Chronic fatigue syndrome (CFS) is a long-lasting condition sometimes associated with the Epstein-Barr virus. It usually first becomes apparent following a bad run-in with the flu. The tiredness and loss of energy just don't go away. You experience recurrent bouts of fever and sore throat and may show heightened susceptibility to other illnesses.

A number of the symptoms also parallel those found in people experiencing the major depression associated with seasonal affective disorder. Sleep problems, fatigue, weakness and pain of the muscles, headaches, irritability, confusion and forgetfulness are common to both. The major difference lies in the fact that the symptoms of CFS continue year round, but the symptoms of SAD are seasonal.

**The importance of obtaining an accurate diagnosis can't be stressed enough.** People with CFS are in the unhappy position of suffering from an illness that, at present, is poorly understood and has no specific course of treatment. People with SAD *can* find relief from their symptoms — in light therapy, lifestyle changes and/or medication.

Dr. Lam of the Mood Disorders Clinic at Vancouver Hospital reports having administered light therapy to two individuals who struggled with depression for years under the misapprehension they had CFS when, in fact, they had SAD. In both cases the light therapy quickly and effectively lifted the depression and associated symptoms.

## Case Study: RALPH

A few years ago, Ralph, an artist in his late forties, came down with what looked to be the flu in November. Most of his symptoms cleared up after one week, but he still felt drained of energy and inclined to sleep an undue amount. Ralph's doctor had him tested for the Epstein-Barr virus and, when the test came back positive, diagnosed Ralph as having chronic fatigue syndrome — a condition that can go on for years.

But much to Ralph's delight, his fatigue and hypersomnia magically disappeared the following summer. He was under the impression he had recovered from CFS when, in October, he became depressed and anxious, started sleeping more than 12 hours a day, lost more than ten pounds and began entertaining fleeting thoughts of suicide. In fact, things got so bad Ralph had to give up his job and obtain professional counselling. It had not occurred to Ralph that his symptoms were following a seasonal pattern, but when treated with two weeks of light therapy, he began to feel almost as well as he had the previous summer.

*— based on Dr. Raymond Lam's clinical research*

# CHAPTER 4

# Mood Disorder Patterns

**R**EFER TO THE SEASONALITY CURVES from the SAD self-assessment in the first chapter (p. 10). Look at the curve that assesses which times of year you feel best and worst. Does your curve show only dips of depression or are there also "feel best" months in which you actually feel better than normal?

*Note: It is only natural to feel good about yourself and your environment once the oppressive symptoms of seasonal affective disorder abate. This sense of well-being should not be confused with the more pronounced emotional symptoms of mania.*

## Spring Swing: The Up Side of Bipolar Disorder

If you are a winter SAD person, you can't wait for spring to arrive. The flowers come up, the trees bud leaves, you can smell the freshly defrosted soil, and there is warmth in the sunshine. Who (aside from someone with summer SAD) wouldn't feel a sense of optimism and well-being? But for those with winter SAD, it's more. Spring is the season when you emerge from the doldrums of depression, shed some of the weight you gained over the winter, get up at a "decent" hour (quite uncoaxed), and finally regain some energy to DO THINGS. Your fancy might even "lightly turn to thoughts of love," as Alfred, Lord Tennyson so aptly noted. You have made it through another brutal winter and have every right to feel good about yourself and the sunny surroundings.

But what happens if you not only regain your original nondepressed state of mind but overshoot the mark? What happens if your level of euphoria continues to grow, perhaps to an unhealthy level? What if you slide into the exaggerated euphoria of hypomania or into the

 **CLINICALLY SPEAKING**          **Bipolar and Recurrent Depressions**

People with seasonal affective disorder are diagnosed as displaying one of two patterns of depression: bipolar and recurrent. If you swing back and forth between depression and a sense of exaggerated euphoria on a seasonal basis, you fall into the *bipolar mood disorder* group. Your mood is polarized into two extremes of behavior and you fluctuate from one to the other during the year.

In contrast to bipolar mood disorder is *recurrent depression*. If you are in this group, you encounter bouts of depression on a seasonal basis, but, when that season is over, you revert to your original state of mind. You don't overshoot your original, "normal" state of mind, as bipolar depressives do.

The category of bipolar depression is usually broken down into two subcategories based on just how far you overshoot on the "feeling good" side of things. Do you simply feel elated and giggle a bit more than usual or do you lose control and engage in totally inappropriate activities? Someone who exdangerous, uncontrollable behavior of full-blown mania, as happens in some instances? How do your friends react when you monopolize conversations or make yourself the center of attention at parties? What happens to your bank account as you indiscriminately buy up anything that catches your fancy? How does your spouse respond when you suddenly have an insatiable appetite for sex after months of total lack of interest? And what happens to your relationship if, in your manic state of mind, you go elsewhere for satisfaction?

periences exaggerated euphoria and a bit of giddiness has "bipolar II" disorder. Someone whose ability to function normally is seriously hindered has "bipolar I" disorder. Another term used for someone in this last subcategory is *manic-depressive*.

When the prevalence of bipolar and recurrent depression among winter and summer SAD sufferers is compared, winter SADs are twice as likely to fall into the bipolar category than summer SADs.

COMMON PATTERNS OF MOOD SWING

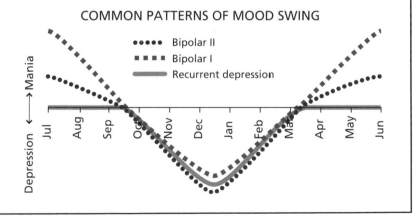

The Spring Swing is not to be taken lightly. It can be every bit as destructive a factor in your life as the severe depression of winter. The onset of mania usually takes place in the month of April for people with winter SAD and September for people with summer SAD. In fact, this April manic peak coincides quite well with the seasonal pattern of hospital admission for mania among the general public. Levels of admission are highest during the spring and summer, drop during the fall and reach their lowest point in the winter. Interestingly, admission of men is greatest in March, April and May, whereas mania admissions for women peak in July.

Again, the number of hours of available sunshine affects the onset of Spring Swing. Studies have shown that both monthly total hours of sunshine and day length correlate significantly with admission rates for mania. Once the days are long enough and the skies are clear a sufficient amount of the time, mania can set in almost immediately.

It is difficult for a person in the midst of mania to recognize and acknowledge the fact. Before spring arrives, have someone close to you — a friend or spouse who is familiar with your normal, non-affected behavior — read up on the tell-tale signs of mania outlined in Chapter 15. It will be comforting to know there is a knowledgeable, objective person looking out for your best interests who can help obtain medical assistance should you require it.

# CHAPTER 5

# Who Gets SAD?

**A**S A MEMBER OF THE GENERAL POPU-lation, you stand slightly more than 1 chance in 100 of being *clinically* affected by SAD over the course of your lifetime. Odds of 1:100 may not seem high but this figure is a *statistical* average. As such, it does not reflect the fact you are far more likely to be

---

### Case Study: OLIE

Olie, a 62-year-old ex-telephone company employee, was diagnosed with SAD five years ago. But looking farther back, Olie figures he actually began suffering from the syndrome about 10 years ago.

"It hits every Labor Day weekend, almost to the day, and doesn't go away until May or June," says Olie. **"By the time I was diagnosed, I'd gone through this routine of feeling bad most of the year for such a long time, I just figured it was natural to feel that way."**

Olie has been treated with various drugs since his diagnosis. At one point he found it difficult to perform his job because the drug he was taking sedated him. "I decided to go through a winter without medications," says Olie, "but my family found me too hard to live with so my wife insisted I go back on medication the next winter."

---

struck by SAD if you are a woman in the prime of life with a family history of mood disorders or alcoholism.

People can suffer the symptoms of SAD at any age. Children and teens, young adults, the middle-aged and seniors all show up in SAD clinics. However, most SAD patients tend to be between the ages of 20 and 40 years. For some, this is when they first experience the onset of SAD; others have been going along experiencing mild symptoms on and off during their childhood or adolescence but it is only now, in the prime of life, that their symptoms become severe enough to present a problem. SAD can be a lifelong ailment in some, but many find it goes away as they age. You might even find you don't experience SAD every year. On average, SAD strikes only seven years out of every ten.

# Women Outnumber Men

Seasonal affective disorder appears to be far more common among women than men. The exact ratio of female to male SAD sufferers varies widely from study to study, but overall, the figure of four females to every male SAD victim has gained general acceptance. This weighting comes as no surprise to the medical community. Females outnumber males in general when it comes to mood disorders.

Or so it would appear!

A random survey of New York residents, which guaranteed anonymity for the respondents and avoided any mention of psychiatry or mental health, found equal numbers of males and females reported symptoms corresponding to either seasonal blues or full-blown SAD. This finding supports a growing suspicion that men might be equally prone to SAD but, due to social pressures, are not as willing as women to admit having mood problems.

Something else might be complicating the issue. People who suffer from SAD fall into two main categories: those who experience only depression and those who vacillate between depression and some degree of mania. In at least one study, it has been found that the 4:1 ratio of women to men holds true for SAD people who exhibit only depression, while the ratio is closer to 3:2 for those who swing between depression and mania.

# Children are Also Affected

People under 20 years of age are by no means immune to seasonal affective disorder. In retrospect, many adult SAD patients can trace the initial onset of their symptoms back to childhood or adolescence.

Children and teenagers with seasonal affective disorder display a set of symptoms similar but not identical to those of adults. Often these include irritability, sadness, decreased ability to concentrate, crying, worrying, fatigue and decreased activity during the winter months. Relationships with family and friends deteriorate, school grades plummet and self-esteem can hit a dangerous low.

Unlike SAD adults, SAD children and teens usually are not plagued by overactive appetites and excessive sleepiness — or at least no more so than other people their age! They do, however, have to battle a constant lack of energy. While their friends are taking part in winter sports activities, going to dances and generally

## Case Study: MAUREEN

Maureen's SADness has been with her a very long time. She remembers being at the top of her class every fall in grade school. After Christmas, her report cards would read "lack of interest — not trying."

Maureen was 19 when it first became obvious something was terribly wrong. She was in her first year of university and had done well during the fall term. Then depression set in and it took Maureen until May to get back on her feet.

Following eight or nine years during which she was blue to one degree or another, Maureen suffered another episode of major depression in 1980. Her family doctor put her on a tricyclic antidepressant that worked but caused unacceptable side effects, so a number of other drugs were tried.

Over the next eight or nine years, Maureen went to an assortment of doctors and psychiatrists trying to find a way off the drugs — to no avail. Every time she eased up on her medications, she relapsed. At this point, Maureen's depression was showing up in varying degrees year round, but most strongly in winter. She read an article in the newspaper about seasonal affective disorder and the local SAD clinic — and, suddenly, everything clicked into place. (Read about Maureen's successful treatment in Chapter 8, p. 91.)

bouncing off the walls, SAD children withdraw to their rooms in frustration.

When spring arrives, like magic, these children begin to perk up and function on an even keel again. Their improved mood can even go a bit overboard. The Spring Swing is seen in greater energy levels and a tendency to talk, talk, talk the summer away.

The diagnosis of childhood SAD can be difficult or deceptive. Many of the symptoms are common to those seen in other disorders. For example, imagine over the past few weeks your child has displayed a severe inability to see a simple task through to completion. He has been venting his frustration by snapping angry remarks at any hapless soul who accidentally crosses his path. Does he have seasonal affective disorder, attention deficit disorder or something else altogether? It has been found that children and teens with SAD respond to light therapy as well as adults. But what if it's not SAD underlying your child's situation? A professional diagnosis is crucial.

# Family Predisposition

Then again, you may be in no state of mind to deal with your child's problems. Seasonal affective disorder appears to run in families. It is not at all unusual for SAD people to have at least one close relative who has suffered depressive episodes and other symptoms associated with SAD over the years.

If it's fall or winter, you and your offspring could all be in the seasonal doldrums. Mood disorders tend to run in families, handed down from one generation to the next. Yet another factor plays a role in your chance of inheriting seasonal affective disorder. Current research shows people with SAD are more likely to have a history of alcoholism in their family than people who suffer from other forms of nonseasonal affective disorder.

# Myopia

In studies headed by Dr. Chris Gorman in Calgary, a higher prevalence of myopia, or nearsightedness, has been found among people with SAD than among non-SAD people.

It has not yet been determined exactly why this should be the case, but one of two factors might come into play. Nearsightedness is caused by an elongation of the eyeball. Light entering the eye comes to a focus just short of the light-sensing photoreceptors of the retina. Perhaps these photoreceptors at the back of the myopic eye do not detect and process light to the same

---

**Case Study: CARLA**

Carla was 21 when she first became clinically depressed, but she has suffered from SAD since childhood. Psychiatric problems run in her family. Carla's paternal grandmother has been a manic-depressive all her life, her mother attempted suicide at 27 years of age and Carla has a cousin in Vancouver, British Columbia who has SAD.

degree as in the normal eye. Alternatively, there is the issue of corrective lenses. Might it be the case that glasses or contact lenses prevent adequate amounts of a critical component of light from reaching the eye? Considerably more research needs to be done in this area before these questions can be answered.

# PART 2

# What Makes You SAD?

# CHAPTER 6

# Some SAD Places

**T**HE SYMPTOMS OF SEASONAL AFFECTIVE disorder are brought on by external triggers in our environment. In the case of winter SAD, the primary trigger is inadequate exposure to light. Lack of sufficient sunshine during the winter months, a work or home environment seriously deficient in natural and artificial light sources, even a local weather pattern with a lot of cloudy days can singly or in combination contribute to the onset of winter SAD symptoms. In the case of summer SAD, the main triggers are heat and

humidity so, once again, the seasonal weather conditions where you live are a significant consideration.

How close is your home to the North Pole? In spite of the fact the top of the world is the legendary home of the jolly elf, the closer you live to

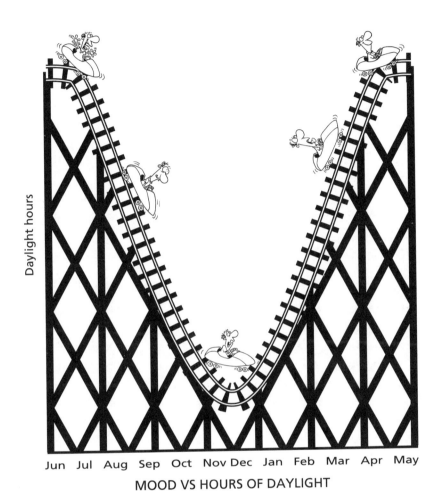

Daylight hours

Jun  Jul  Aug  Sep  Oct  Nov Dec  Jan  Feb  Mar  Apr  May

**MOOD VS HOURS OF DAYLIGHT**

good old Santa, the more likely you are to be SAD in winter. We all know about those endless winter nights above the Arctic Circle. Unlike Santa, most of us are fortunate enough to see some sunshine during the winter. However, the shorter the hours of winter daylight, the higher the probability is you will succumb to SAD.

How far north you live determines how drastically you see the number of daylight hours diminish toward the end of the year. If you live in Toronto, Ontario, you are illuminated by sunlight for just under nine hours on the shortest day of the year, the winter solstice, which usually falls on the 20th or 21st of December. On that same day, a person living in Dallas, Texas, gets 10 hours of solar exposure and someone living above the Arctic Circle is surrounded by dark the entire 24 hours.

## Total Hours of Daylight on the Shortest Day of the Year

| City | Latitude North | Daylight Hours |
| --- | --- | --- |
| Fairbanks, Alaska | 65° 00' | 3 hrs. 42 mins. |
| Anchorage, Alaska | 61° 10' | 5 hrs. 28 mins. |
| Edmonton, Alberta | 53° 33' | 7 hrs. 27 mins. |
| Calgary, Alberta | 51° 03' | 7 hrs. 43 mins. |
| Vancouver, British Columbia | 49° 51' | 8 hrs. 11 mins. |
| Seattle, Washington | 47° 36' | 8 hrs. 16 mins. |
| Montreal, Quebec | 45° 31' | 8 hrs. 42 mins. |
| Minneapolis, Minnesota | 44° 59' | 8 hrs. 46 mins. |
| Toronto, Ontario | 43° 39' | 8 hrs. 56 mins. |
| Milwaukee, Wisconsin | 43° 02' | 9 hrs. 00 mins. |
| Detroit, Michigan | 42° 20' | 9 hrs. 04 mins. |
| Chicago, Illinois | 41° 56' | 9 hrs. 08 mins. |
| Salt Lake City, Utah | 40° 45' | 9 hrs. 15 mins. |
| San Francisco, California | 37° 46' | 9 hrs. 33 mins. |
| Los Angeles, California | 34° 03' | 9 hrs. 46 mins. |
| Houston, Texas | 29° 46' | 10 hrs. 14 mins. |
| Miami, Florida | 25° 47' | 10 hrs. 26 mins. |
| Honolulu, Hawaii | 21° 18' | 10 hrs. 50 mins. |

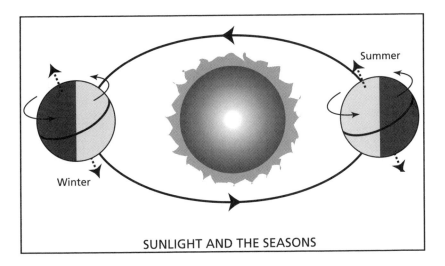

**SUNLIGHT AND THE SEASONS**

What brings about this lopsided distribution of daylight? A lopsided planet, of course! The earth spins around an axis through the North and South poles. If this axis of rotation were oriented straight up and down with respect to the plane of the earth's orbit, we would have equal hours of night and day all year long. Instead, the axis is tilted off to one side by 23.5°.

As the earth travels around the sun, the extreme north and south regions of the planet are alternately pointed away from the sun at different times of the year. In the northern hemisphere, our pole is pointed away from the sun in winter, hence the fewer hours of daily sunlight and the onset of SAD at this time of year. In the southern hemisphere, the South Pole is pointed away from the sun six months later. If you live at an extreme southern latitude, say in Buenos Aires, your SAD symptoms will set in at this time of year.

The correlation between short mid-winter daylight periods and SAD in the far North has been demonstrated by researchers in Fairbanks, Alaska. This city is at 65°N latitude and has an annual variation in daylight hours from 3 hours 42 minutes at the winter solstice to a whopping 21 hours 49 minutes of sunshine at the summer solstice.

A survey of Fairbanks has come up with some interesting data on SAD. Slightly more than 28 percent of Fairbanks residents surveyed are affected to some degree by SAD. That's more than one person in four. Over 9 percent fall into the full-blown SAD category while roughly 19 percent suffer the winter blues. As in studies carried out elsewhere, the prevalence of SAD appears to drop off in the segment of Fairbanks' population over 40 years of age. But unlike the situation at more southern latitudes, the ratio of SAD women to SAD men is much lower, coming in at 3:2 rather than the more widely seen 4:1.

At the other end of the spectrum, a study of the occurrence of SAD in four different cities along the eastern seaboard of the United States found that only four percent of the residents of Sarasota, Florida (at latitude 27°N) suffered from either clinical SAD (1.4%) or the winter blues (2.6%).

Comparative studies such as these demonstrate another trend that goes hand in hand with increasing latitude. The longer the winter season, the longer the duration of SAD episodes. In Alaska, it is common to see SAD symptoms run from late September through until March. Further south it is more common to see episodes last from November to February. There are even some relatively fortunate individuals who only have to tough out the months of January and February.

# SAD Weather Cities

See if this sounds familiar. You are walking along the street on a beautiful sunny day. It's spring and you are feeling better than you've felt for months. You breathe in the warm, floral-scented air and cast your gaze around at the pleasant greening scenery. You expect to be calmed and refreshed by the sight and, for the most part, you are. But out on the far edge of your conscious-ness a tiny warning flag has gone up. Something isn't quite right.

The warning signal isn't strong enough to demand attention, so you continue on your way — for a while. Suddenly it's back, this time as a real and present sense that something is wrong. Puzzled, you look around. And, sure enough, there is the problem. A flotilla of dense cloud is slowly advancing toward your position, threatening to darken your day and your spirits. The same sense of mild panic you experience during the dwindling days of fall sets in. You head back to the of-fice or your house thankful that you got out into the sunshine while it was still around and you do your best to mentally prepare yourself for the gloom about to descend.

A long run of cloudy weather can trigger onset of the symptoms of seasonal affective disorder, even in the middle of summer. Fortunately, these nonseasonal bouts of SAD are temporary, clearing within a few days of the return of sunny skies. (Likewise, several days of clear, sunny weather in the midst of winter can give your spirits a temporary boost while you are plodding through this bleak time of year.)

Some cities are notorious for their long stretches of dark, cloudy weather. Both Vancouver, British Columbia and Seattle, Washington make us think of rain. Other cities are famous for their clear winter skies. Winnipeg, Manitoba, tops the list of Canadian cities with the greatest number of hours of sunshine during the three-month period of December, January and February. Granted, in January the atmosphere over Winnipeg is often too *cold* to retain moisture in the form of clouds, but it is sunny!

## Case Study: MARGE

Eight years ago Marge left the Detroit area, moved to Calgary and succumbed to SAD the very next winter. "Down East, winter only seems to last from December to the end of February — too short a period to affect me," says Marge. She blames her annual bouts of depression on Calgary's longer hours of darkness during the winter and relatively cool summers, going as far as to claim with great vehemence, "We don't have summers here!"

The weather pattern in your region can play an important role in the effect SAD has on your life. Cloud and sunshine are factors in the case of winter SAD. Heat and humidity are reported triggers for summer SAD. The charts on pages 76 and 77 will tell you how selected cities in Canada and the United States shape up in these regards.

If you have winter SAD, you want maximum hours of winter sunshine and minimum hours of overcast sky.

Beware cities that are sunnier than average during the winter but cloudy the rest of the year.

If you have summer SAD, you might want to avoid Windsor, Ontario, during June, July and August. It ranks as *the* most humid city in Canada and also as one of the three hottest cities in Canada.

Several southern U.S. holiday destinations have been included in the chart to aid you in vacation travel planning.

# SAD Buildings

Do you live in a house or apartment lacking in windows, especially south-facing? Do you work in a windowless building or spend most of your day at a work station so far removed from a source of natural light that you might as well be working the night shift? Perhaps you *do* work the night shift.

If your lifestyle keeps you tucked away all day in the modern equivalent of a cave, something has to change! As you will see in Part 3, a mere half hour exposure to sunshine on a daily basis is often enough to ward off the onset of SAD symptoms. You might need more. The exact amount varies from person to person. The question is, are you getting the daily dose of sunshine your body requires?

A limited amount of research has been carried out on the issue of how much time the typical urbanite spends outside on a daily basis. The study quoted most widely is one conducted by Dr. Thomas J. Savides. He attached devices to the foreheads of ten young adult volunteers and monitored how much time each spent indoors and outdoors every day.

When he analyzed the results, he found that most of the participants exhibited one of two extremes of behavior. All ten were medical students. Those who kept their nose to the grindstone averaged 26 minutes of exposure to bright outdoor light daily, much less than the four hours of daily exposure chalked up by the fitness buffs among them.

A similar study focused on a group of healthy elderly people found they averaged about one hour of bright light exposure daily. Based on this and Dr. Savides' study, it appears urbanites get out into the sunshine somewhere between one and one and a half hours per day, on average. There's just one problem with this picture. Both studies were carried out in sunny, warm San Diego, California. What might the results have looked like if this research had been done during January in Toronto?

One interesting statistic that came out of these studies is the fact that overall, the men got three times as much exposure to bright light as the women. More than a few people have questioned whether this difference might have something to do with the higher occurrence of SAD among women.

If you estimate your daily bright-light exposure, especially during winter months, you might be genuinely surprised by the results. Do you get anywhere near one hour of sunshine per day, as the urbanites in the San Diego study averaged? Do you get even a half hour of exposure to sunshine per day, the equivalent of bright-light therapy (see Chapter 8)? Here's a mental exercise you can adapt to your own situation.

Let's assume "Tom" lives in Toronto, one of the southernmost cities in Canada. It is December 21, the shortest day of the year, and he is off to work. His job begins at 8:30 a.m., so he leaves the house at 7:45, exactly two minutes before the sun pops up on the eastern horizon.

After half an hour the sun is high enough to provide a significant dose of light. At this point Tom is 13 minutes away from the office. Okay. That's 13 minutes of bright-light exposure, assuming it's a clear day and assuming Tom is not spending his time in the bowels of the subway system!

During his lunch break, he ducks in and out of various shops, gaining another five minutes light exposure along the way. Finally, it is 4:30. His work day is over and the sun is already too low in the West to do him any good. Another 13 minutes and it will have set.

Tom's total bright-light exposure for the day? Eighteen minutes — nowhere near enough light to fend off the winter blues, let alone full-blown SAD.

## Canadian SAD Weather Stats

| City | Hours of Sunshine (Dec.– Feb.) | Hours/Yr. Overcast Sky (80% or more) | Avg. Max. Temp.(°C) (June– Aug.) | Avg. Humidity in kPa (June– Aug.) |
|---|---|---|---|---|
| Calgary | 353 | 4271 | 22.2 | 1.01 |
| Charlottetown | 284 | 4545 | 21.7 | 1.52 |
| Churchill | 253 | 4984 | 14.5 | 0.94 |
| Edmonton | 289 | 4581 | 22.1 | 1.17 |
| Goose Bay | 295 | 5406 | 19.0 | 1.08 |
| Halifax | 336 | 5075 | 22.2 | 1.49 |
| Kamloops | 197 | 3757 | 27.3 | 1.10 |
| Montréal | 306 | 4718 | 24.7 | 1.61 |
| Ottawa-Hull | 313 | 4357 | 24.9 | 1.53 |
| Prince George | 188 | 5258 | 21.1 | 1.05 |
| Prince Rupert | 141 | 6123 | 15.5 | 1.23 |
| Québec City | 305 | 4894 | 23.4 | 1.47 |
| Regina | 315 | 3923 | 25.1 | 1.20 |
| Saint John | 338 | 4863 | 21.0 | 1.40 |
| St. John's | 223 | 5916 | 18.5 | 1.28 |
| Saskatoon | 322 | 3792 | 24.3 | 1.18 |
| Sault Ste. Marie | 247 | 3964 | 22.6 | 1.44 |
| Thunder Bay | 342 | 4643 | 22.6 | 1.36 |
| Toronto | 281 | 4528 | 25.1 | 1.59 |
| Victoria | 210 | 4688 | 21.0 | 1.28 |
| Vancouver | 195 | 5240 | 20.9 | 1.40 |
| Whitehorse | 168 | 5067 | 18.9 | 0.85 |
| Windsor | Not avail. | 4688 | 26.5 | 1.78 |
| Winnipeg | 358 | 4115 | 24.8 | 1.42 |
| Yellowknife | Not avail. | 4405 | 19.0 | 0.99 |

## U.S. SAD Weather Stats

| City | Cloudy Days Per Year (Max. = 365) | Sunny Days (Dec. - Feb.) (Max. = 90) | Avg. Max. Temp. (°F) (June–Aug.) |
|---|---|---|---|
| Billings | 152 | 43 | 84 |
| Boise | 146 | 33 | 86 |
| Boston | 160 | 47 | 79 |
| Buffalo | 192 | 25 | 79 |
| Chicago | 167 | 39 | 82 |
| Cleveland | 188 | 26 | 83 |
| Denver | 115 | 59 | 86 |
| Detroit | 178 | 30 | 82 |
| Duluth | 182 | 40 | 74 |
| Fairbanks | 205 | 43 | 69 |
| Fargo | 161 | 43 | 81 |
| Honolulu | 264 | 61 | 85 |
| Houston | 147 | 43 | 92 |
| Las Vegas | 65 | 60 | 102 |
| Los Angeles | 74 | 64 | 81 |
| Miami | 104 | 69 | 89 |
| Minneapolis | 160 | 45 | 82 |
| Nashville | 151 | 38 | 89 |
| New York City | 130 | 53 | 80 |
| Omaha | 141 | 48 | 86 |
| Orlando | 118 | 63 | 90 |
| Philadelphia | 160 | 46 | 85 |
| Phoenix | 72 | 62 | 103 |
| Pittsburgh | 198 | 28 | 81 |
| Portland | 229 | 15 | 76 |
| St. Louis | 131 | 45 | 87 |
| Salt Lake City | 123 | 42 | 88 |
| San Francisco | 96 | 59 | 65 |
| Seattle | 229 | 18 | 73 |
| Spokane | 188 | 22 | 81 |
| Tucson | 79 | 62 | 98 |
| Washington, D.C. | 158 | 44 | 85 |

# CHAPTER 7

# Factors That Compound SADness

**H**AVE YOU EVER NOTICED HOW THE main characters in television shows are faced with a single, isolated crisis to overcome in each episode? Wouldn't it be nice if life were like that? Wouldn't it be great if you could direct all your energy into the battle against the winter blues when it hit and ignore other problems until your SADness lifted?

Unfortunately, seasonal affective disorder sufferers are usually in the midst of multiple, real-world crunches when their symptoms set in. There are no simple, one-episode solutions at hand. They must forge ahead and cope as best they can with SAD and any number of other problems all at once.

Things really begin to get dicey when these factors interact and compound one another's effects. Sometimes problems, such as stress, worsen the symptoms of seasonal affective disorder. At other times, the presence of SAD intensifies the symptoms of physical conditions such as premenstrual syndrome.

## Stress

In today's North American culture, is there a single person who has never experienced stress? From the peer pressure and exam anxiety of grade school to the tough management decisions and deadlines of the workplace, stress is a lifelong companion.

Even if you are the most calm, level-headed stress handler in town most of the year, when SAD sets in, you likely find it exceedingly difficult to cope with adverse or frustrating situations. The opposite holds true as well. Even if you are managing your seasonal affective disorder or seasonal blues quite successfully, it is possible for a stressful situation to up and blindside you, bringing on depression in all its fury.

## Case Study: BURTON

Burton was born and raised in the mountains of British Columbia. He actually *liked* winter. Then nine or ten years ago, he developed a decided "intolerance" for the season, tending to sleep all the time he wasn't up binging on carbohydrates and growling at his family.

"Things got worse over the years, as my middle-management position as a psychiatric nurse became more stressful," says Burton. "But after I went on light therapy, I was once again able to handle the stress and make decisions. **It was like someone had switched the light on inside me.**"

One thing Burton claims has been very useful is a diary he has kept in the form of a calendar. "I write how I feel and what the weather is like in the space allotted for each day," explains Burton. "It's given both me and my doctor a better idea of what's going on."

Imagine it is mid-January. You are juggling as many activities and commitments as you feel you are up to handling. You're dragging along, but you have everything under control — until your car is stolen. At this point, a non-SAD person would probably use a few choice words, call the police and the car's insurer, then get on with arranging alternate transportation. In contrast, you are overwhelmed. This is too much to bear. Why *your* car? Why now? You become despondent, withdraw and fail to see the point in making the effort to "cope." Your SADness worsens.

Some stress factors in our lives are as seasonal as SAD. You can see them coming months in advance. And in combination with your SAD condition, they can create major potholes of depression you might find yourself stumbling into over and over again. Here are a few examples.

• Every year, beginning in mid-November, the pressure of holiday season starts to build. There are gifts to buy, cards to get into the mail, parties to throw and attend, out-of-town visitors to accommodate. By the end of December, even a non-SAD person tends to feel fatigued and a bit spaced out. For someone with winter SAD, this can be a devastating time of year. You are too depressed to socialize, too out of oomph to go out and shop, too unfocused to plan family get-togethers. And yet, you feel all these things are expected of you. The stress factor is enormous.

• If you are a winter SAD student, you face struggling through mid-year examinations at the worst possible time. For the past several weeks you have been unable to concentrate on your studies. Just making it

## Case Study: CRAWFORD

The debilitating effects of SAD got Crawford thrown out of university. "In the fall every year, I would begin having problems functioning normally," says Crawford. "In Civil Engineering, my major, you had to work with your classmates on assignments, and the withdrawal brought on by SAD didn't make this easy. I would begin to worry and become even more depressed and unable to manage the work load. My grades were terrible and, eventually, I was thrown out of university."

Crawford and his doctor are in the process of finding the treatment most effective for him and, when they do, he hopes to tackle university studies once more. Crawford has proof he possesses the innate skill and knowledge to handle university work. "One year I took classes in the spring and summer and did fantastically," he claims.

to school has been a real challenge. And staying awake to jot down lecture notes during class? Dream on! Now it's exam time. You feel it is entirely your fault you are not better prepared. You feel inadequate, worthless. The whole exercise is hopeless. And the more pressure you put on yourself to do well in the face of it, the more disappointed and depressed you become. The only bright note is that you will have a chance to redeem your grades on the final exam in spring, when you are feeling better.

• In the United States, March brings the frustration of filling out income tax forms and the stress of meeting your financial situation head on. In Canada, the same holds true in April. If you are not out of your winter blues by this time, the stress might be enough to further dampen your spirits. This, in turn, can postpone remission of your SAD symptoms.

The three above examples apply to many North Americans. Other seasonal rough spots can be of a personal nature and totally unique to you. For example, it is common to become depressed or agitated every year on or around the anniversary date of a disturbing incident from your past — the death of a close family member or friend, the occurrence of a serious accident, even the loss of a pet. You may feel out-of-sorts because the anniversary date is at hand or subtle clues in your environment unconsciously trigger the onset of your reaction at this time of year. Either way, you are in for an emotional ambush every year on cue.

Any one of these seasonal stressors can bring about depression, regardless of whether or not you suffer from seasonal affective disorder. Because of this, social stresses that recur on a seasonal basis are not taken into account in the diagnosis of SAD. Many SAD researchers have questioned the wisdom of this approach, arguing these stress factors are valid as trigger mechanisms and should not be entirely dismissed from the picture.

# Premenstrual Syndrome

If you are a woman who suffers from premenstrual syndrome (PMS), you may be thinking that SAD sounds like what you experience with PMS. Every month, beginning a week or two before your period, you start craving sweets and high-carbohydrate foods. You lose all your get-up-and-go and prefer to stay in bed, away from everyone else. And everyone else would just as soon you did. "Grouch" is a mild term for the way you come across during this part of your cycle.

While irritability is not generally associated with the depression of seasonal affective disorder (although it can show up as a component of childhood and summer SAD), the symptoms and cyclic nature of SAD and PMS are remarkably comparable.

The preliminary results of research carried out by Dr. Barbara Parry and her colleagues in the Department of Psychiatry at the University of California, San Diego, indicate light therapy might be effective against the symptoms of PMS. If this proves to be the case, those who suffer from both SAD and PMS may be able to kill two birds with one stone.

# Panic Attacks

A recent study conducted by Dr. Mark T. Halle of Ohio State University and Dr. Steven C. Dilsaver of Harris County Psychiatric Center, Houston, looked at the prevalence of panic disorder among patients with winter SAD. They found nearly 24 percent, almost one in four, SAD patients are susceptible to panic attacks. These panic attacks come on every fall or winter at the same time as their SAD depression and clear up spontaneously in the spring, along with the symptoms of their seasonal affective disorder. Halle and Dilsaver conclude that winter SAD people appear to be in a high-risk category for the simultaneous onset of panic disorder.

Now that you understand the *who, what, where* and *when* of seasonal affective disorder, move on to Part 3 and see *how* you can overcome the effects of SAD and regain control of your life. (We'll look at why people are SAD in Part 4.)

## Case Study: Forgetful JEAN

**"SAD was taking my life away from me,"** exclaims Jean (see Chapter 1). "I have only isolated memories of events that occurred between November and the end of February during the years before I got treatment. I can't remember Christmas at all from that time period."

Jean's poor memory made it extremely difficult to go outside during bouts of depression. "I simply COULD NOT do Christmas shopping. Anxiety over whether I would have a memory lapse in the middle of the mall put me under such stress that I had panic attacks when I did venture out."

# PART 3

# Don't Be SAD!

**N**OW FOR THE GOOD NEWS. IN THE FOL-
lowing pages you will read about not one but
several ways you can go about banishing
SAD and the seasonal blues.

The most fascinating and unconventional treatment
for seasonal affective disorder is the totally painless
technique known as *light therapy*. It was initially developed by Dr. Norman Rosenthal and his colleagues, the
same people who put SAD on the map in 1984. During
the past decade, researchers in clinics around the world
have tested, modified and quantified light therapy.
Much has been learned about the mechanism of light
starvation through the use of this powerful tool. It

clearly provides a curative effect for people with SAD. And yet a great deal of controversy remains. Chapter 8 discusses why.

Another popular route to relief is through anti-depressant medication. Like light therapy, it must be taken under the supervision of your physician. There are many different drugs that can be prescribed. We'll sum up the benefits and drawbacks of the ones used most widely so you can come to an informed decision in consultation with your doctor.

Certain lifestyle changes can enhance and reinforce the improvement you gain from light therapy and/or medication. The exercise, diet, decorating and travel suggestions in this section may be sufficient to lift you out of the milder seasonal blues.

# CHAPTER 8

# Light Therapy: Coming Out of the Dark Ages

L IGHT THERAPY, SOMETIMES CALLED *phototherapy*, is truly amazing. In one week or less, it often can reduce severe winter SAD symptoms, which sometimes go completely into remission.

Response to light therapy varies considerably. One person might find light therapy clears up his overwhelming urge to sleep 13 hours a day but does nothing to blunt his appetite for sweets. Another person might see her eating binges diminish hand in hand with her weight problem while she is taking light therapy. Overall, light therapy proves effective for 60 to 70 percent of people who try it.

## Will Light Therapy Help?

Is there some way of predicting who is likely to respond to light therapy and who is not? Dr. Raymond Lam in Vancouver has found that young SAD people who suffer from oversleeping and increased appetite respond exceptionally well to morning light therapy. Other studies confirm that hypersomnia and a tendency to consume large amounts of sweet foods late in the day are both excellent indicators of winter SAD individuals who can expect to benefit significantly from light therapy.

If you don't meet any of these criteria, you may still respond well to light therapy. **These are only general guidelines.** Every SAD person is different and, given the ease and rapid effect of light therapy, it is well worth trying as your first line of defense.

A high percentage of light therapy recipients begin to see improvement in their SAD condition after one week of daily treatment. Dr. Norman Rosenthal observes there is evidence to indicate the antidepressant effect of light therapy may increase gradually over several weeks. So if you show no response to light therapy at the one-week mark, you might very well begin to respond during the second or third week. Don't give up too soon!

# Choosing the Right Light Therapy

The information on the following pages will give you some idea of what light therapy is all about and put you in a reasonable position to discuss with your doctor if and how you should go about obtaining light treatment. You basically have two options:

1. You can enter a program administered by a local light therapy clinic.
2. You can self-administer light therapy at home under a doctor's or clinician's supervision.

Consult with a medical professional, your physician or therapist, to see which option is appropriate. For the seasonal blues, home treatment may be enough. On the other hand, if you are severely depressed and unable to cope with a self-regulated program, you may need the extra help a clinic can provide.

Either way, it is important to establish contact with a trained light therapy clinician who can provide advice and encouragement throughout your treatment. Response to light therapy varies a lot. Fine-tuning a program to your specific requirements may be delicate. Professional insights can save you time, minimize frustration and prevent you from overdosing on light (see Side Effects of Light Therapy, p. 104). A list of Canadian and U.S. light therapy clinics and medical practitioners offering treatment for SAD is included in Appendix C along with a list of light therapy equipment suppliers in Appendix E.

# When Should You Use Light Therapy?

This is a double-barreled question. It includes both the time of *year* you should begin light treatments and the time of *day* you should undertake them. Let's look at the time of year first.

You should haul your light unit out of storage, dust it off and have it ready to plug in as soon as your annual SAD symptoms begin to show up in the fall. It can take anywhere from three or four days to two or three weeks for the light therapy to take effect. Why waste more precious time than necessary?

Begin slowly. Supplement the dwindling hours of sunlight with gradually increasing lengths of light treatment. The amount of time you spend in daily light therapy depends on the intensity of your light equipment and your individual needs. As a rule of thumb, you want to work up to two hours per day exposure to 2,500-lux light or 30 minutes exposure to 10,000-lux light, assuming you are using a light box or lamp. If you are using a light visor, work up to 30 minutes exposure, regardless of the unit's light output. And if you are using a dawn simulator, a maximum of two hours exposure should be attained in gradual increments. (These various types of equipment are discussed in the next section.)

Now, at what time of day should you undertake light treatment? Or is there a best time of day? Again, this depends entirely on you. Preliminary studies pooled

## Case Study: MAUREEN Revisited

Maureen (see Chapter 5) followed up on a newspaper article she read about SAD by seeking help from her local light therapy clinic. **"I felt like my battery was running down in November,"** says Maureen. The clinic administered light treatment and it took only four or five days before Maureen saw results.

"The light therapy has had a staggering effect," claims Maureen. "It especially has helped get rid of my fatigue."

Maureen decided to go off light therapy one February. She attempted to replace the treatment by spending more time skiing outdoors in the sunshine, but reports she began to feel her mood going downhill again. "I went back to the lights and presto!"

from around the world initially indicated a much higher remission rate of SAD symptoms when light therapy was administered in the morning, as opposed to the evening. However, this finding has not stood up under closer scrutiny. It is now evident that light therapy can be equally effective at other times of the day. The only exception is late in the evening, when light therapy is likely to inhibit your ability to fall asleep afterward.

# Nuts and Bolts of Light Therapy

During the past 10 years, several devices capable of delivering therapeutic amounts of light to the eyes have been developed and tested in Canada and the United States. The original **light box** is now available in a number of shapes, sizes and intensities. At least two models of **portable light visor** are on the market. And **dawn simulation units** are an exciting new development.

Your form of light therapy depends on a combination of factors: professional advice regarding home versus clinical treatment in your particular situation; the dosage of light that proves effective for you; the form of therapy that meshes best with your lifestyle; and, in many cases, the type of apparatus that lightens your spirits, not your pocketbook.

*Note: If you plan to purchase light therapy equipment, check whether your health insurance will cover the expense.*

# Light Boxes and Lamps

The light box, first pioneered by Dr. Norman Rosenthal and his colleagues at the National Institute of Mental Health (NIMH), has been used extensively in both clinics and homes. Light box units consist of up to eight fluorescent or full-spectrum bulbs mounted in a case covered by a diffusion screen. The original design was a simple rectangular box that sat horizontally atop a table or vertically on the floor, always positioned at eye level. Several variants are now available. There are hinged, folding units that provide greater stability when stood on end. There are light boxes supported on stands

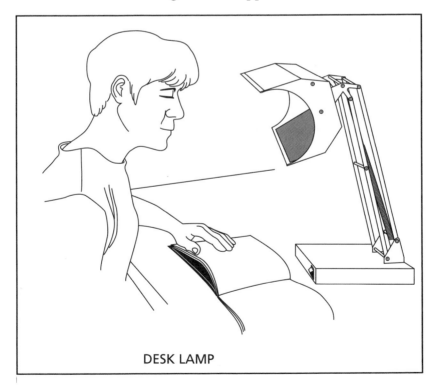

DESK LAMP

that tilt the light down on you at the proper angle to illuminate your eyes yet not be obtrusive. There are even stylish, compact units that look like nothing more than a slightly oversized desk lamp.

Regardless of the light box or lamp design you use, it is critical to position yourself the right distance from the unit in order for the correct amount of light to reach your eyes. Usually this is three feet away for a light box, no more than 17 inches away for the lamp. In the first stages of your treatment you might need to adjust this distance. If you do not respond after two weeks, try moving a little closer. Alternately, if you respond too well and feel yourself slipping into the exaggerated euphoria of Spring Swing, back off a bit. Do not stare directly into the light. Rather, glance into it occasionally. Many people read or perform some other stationary task while basking in its illumination.

The dose of light you receive is defined by the brightness of your light source and the amount of time you are exposed to it. For many years now, the standard light box used in light therapy has been a model that delivers 2,500 lux of light, an intensity much brighter than a well-lit room but still dimmer than outdoor sunshine. More than half the people who sit in front of such units for two hours, the recommended therapeutic dose, benefit substantially. Others require exposure periods much longer than two hours. And some people show no response at all to 2,500-lux treatment, regardless of the number of hours of exposure.

Light units that deliver a much brighter, 10,000-lux or higher light have become available in the last few years. And presto! Many of the people who previously

# An illuminating note regarding lux

You are probably saying to yourself, what on earth is "lux," other than the name of a dishwashing detergent? The technical definition of *lux* can get quite convoluted. For our purposes, we will define the lux unit as a measurement of illumination. In light therapy, lux is used to designate the amount of light falling on your eyes. For example, a single 100-watt incandescent bulb seen from three feet (about 1 meter) away delivers slightly less than 100 lux of light to your eyes. Compare this to the massive doses of 2,500 and 10,000 lux used in most light therapy treatments and it is easy to see that the lighting inside the average home or office falls far short of the SAD person's daily requirement. Here are a few more lux readings for comparison:

| | | |
|---|---|---|
| One 5-ft. (1.5-m) fluorescent tube (at 3-ft. distance) | = | about 400 lux |
| 6-8 closely packed 40-watt bulbs (at 3-ft. distance) | = | about 2,500 lux |
| Ambient light in the average home | = | 200 to 500 lux |
| Ambient light in the average office | = | 400 to 700 lux |
| Ambient light in a drafting room | = | 500 to 1,000 lux |
| Sky at twilight | = | less than 750 lux |
| Sky on bright overcast day (temperate zone) | = | about 10,000 lux |
| Clear sky one half hour after sunrise (temperate zone) | = | about 10,000 lux |
| Clear sky at noon (temperate zone) | = | about 80,000 lux |
| Clear sky at noon (near equator) | = | about 100,000 lux |

showed no improvement using 2,500 lux units now have SAD on the run.

The 10,000-lux light unit provides one other great advantage — shorter treatment sessions. Clinical trials show that, for SAD people favorably disposed to light therapy, only 30 minutes of 10,000-lux light once a day works as well as two hours of 2,500-lux treatment.

# Light Visors

Light visors have evolved from market demand for a truly portable artificial light source. A light box is a large object you tend to leave in place once you set it up and plug it in. During your daily dose of light therapy, you must remain seated in front of it for the duration of your treatment, be that 30 minutes, two hours or longer. How

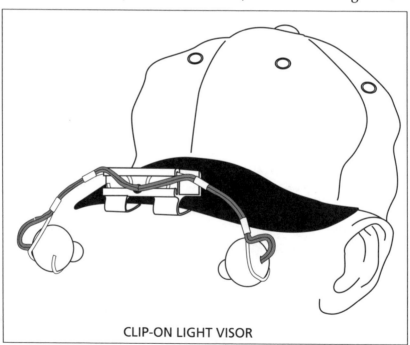

CLIP-ON LIGHT VISOR

many people have the time or patience to stick with a routine that so thoroughly ties them down?

Enter the light visor, a self-contained, battery-operated unit that is worn on the head for 30 minutes per day. The original light visor design is an innovation of SAD investigators at NIMH and Jefferson Medical College. This futuristic-looking head gear has two small incandescent lights built into the brim. Another model has been developed in Canada, which consists of a battery pack and two small light-emitting diodes that can be attached to any baseball-type hat or pair of eyeglasses. The dim lights in these units are focused to shine directly into the upper visual field of your eyes, without obstructing your view.

Dim light? Don't you need to pump mega-photons into your eyes for light therapy to work? Apparently not.

In trial studies, the dim light of visors has alleviated SAD symptoms in 6 or 7 people out of every 10 participants — a success rate fully comparable, if not superior, to light boxes. Head-mounted visors might be more efficient light delivery devices than boxes. When sitting in front of a light box, you involuntarily move your upper body back and forth and unconsciously turn your head away from the light source untold times during a therapy session. Visors keep the light source focused on your eyes at a fixed distance, delivering a more consistent dose of light to your retinas. Perhaps this constancy compensates for the relatively low light output of light visors.

Is intensity the critical factor in light therapy? Could there be some other aspect of light at work in the treatment of SAD?

**The Issue of Intensity**

The beneficial effect of light visors does not vary with the *intensity* of light used. Studies comparing the effectiveness of bright light vs. dim light in visors show that light as dim as 30 lux is nearly as effective as 7,000-lux light when administered for an equal length of time (30 minutes). Given the pronounced relationship between intensity and length of treatment session that holds true for light boxes (2 hours at 2,500 lux versus 30 minutes at 10,000 lux), how can doses of 30 lux and 7,000 lux possibly produce comparable results?

Good question. Dr. Russell Joffe of the Clarke Institute of Psychiatry in Toronto headed a multicenter light visor study that found no significant difference in patient response to 60, 600 and 3,500 lux doses of light. He and his colleagues suggest one of two things might be happening.

Perhaps the placebo effect is at work. (More about placebos later in this chapter.) Perhaps the fact participants are undergoing a novel form of treatment is enough to subconsciously trigger an antidepressant response that has absolutely nothing to do with the quality of light administered. In similar antidepressant trials, the placebo effect has been shown to account for up to 40 percent of positive results.

The alternative explanation suggests that a wide range of light intensities can produce an antidepressant response in people with SAD. Dr. Joffe points out that monochromatic light (light made up of one color) as dim as 29 lux can suppress the brain's production of melatonin, the biochemical that regulates many of our internal rhythms. Should we be surprised when 30-lux light alleviates the depression of SAD?

# Color and Light Therapy

Light is light, right? Not quite. Did you know that cosmetic vanities have incandescent light bulbs to give skin a radiant glow? Perhaps you have purchased an item of clothing or a piece of furniture inside a store lit with fluorescent bulbs only to find your purchase turns an entirely different hue once you get it out in the sunshine? Point made.

In everyday life, we encounter four different sources of light: the sun, incandescent bulbs (this includes halogen lights), fluorescent bulbs and full-spectrum bulbs. If we analyze the color make-up of the light emitted by each source, every color of the rainbow can be detected in all four. What differs from source to source is the relative strength of each color component. Light from incandescent bulbs tends to be dominated by red, whereas fluorescent light is strongest in the blue-green and yellow components. Natural sunlight is robust in all colors but strongest in the blue-green. This is the type of light full-spectrum bulbs are designed to mimic as closely as possible. They strive admirably, but they emit just a bit less red than sunshine.

Research carried out at the National Institute of Mental Health has shown not only the intensity of light but also the color has some bearing on how well light therapy works against seasonal affective disorder. One color stands out as being particularly effective — green. This makes sense; blue-green is the dominant color in sunlight. Photoreceptors in human eyes have evolved to be most sensitive to the color green. Some researchers feel this supports the theory that malfunctioning photoreceptors in the retina of the eye play a major role in the underlying cause of SAD. (More about this in Part 4.)

One component of natural sunlight need not be present in light therapy. In fact, it is quite undesirable. This is ultraviolet light (often referred to as UV). Prolonged exposure to UV can lead to skin cancer and cataracts. Properly constructed light therapy units include a **diffusion screen** to shield you from UV light. Dr. Chris Gorman at Calgary's Foothills Hospital points out that, ironically, as the ozone layer thins and the UV screening effect of the earth's atmosphere diminishes, there might come a time in the near future when exposure to artificial lights is safer than exposure to natural sunlight!

In theory, all three types of artificial light bulb can function successfully in the light boxes used for light therapy — incandescent, fluorescent or full-spectrum. All three bulbs have a green component in the light they emit. Even the red-dominated incandescents put out sufficient green to be effective if used in a strong enough dosage. When outfitting a light box, however, fluorescent or full-spectrum lights are the obvious choice if you want to optimize your exposure to the green component of light.

Visors present a different story. As a potential user, you should be aware of the differences between the two types of visors available, red light and white light.

Much to the surprise of researchers, red light has proven to be extremely effective when used in light visors. Dim red light was originally used in light visor trials as a control element. It had performed so poorly in previous light box trials, it was assumed dim red light was incapable of triggering an antidepressant response. In trial studies of light visors, researchers anticipated that any positive results achieved with dim red light would indicate the level of placebo effect present.

So what does it mean when the control group walks away from a trial in comparable shape to the group receiving treatment? This is exactly what happened in one study that compared light visors equipped with 600-lux white light (the treatment) to visors with 30-lux red light (the control). In another study, dim red light (86-lux) was used as the control opposite bright red light (1,432-lux), yet proved to be equally effective.

Just how dim can red light get and still be effective against SAD? You might be surprised.

# Dawn Simulation Therapy

Dawn simulation is a revolutionary technique you can use while you sleep. You don't even have to open your eyes for this light therapy method to work.

Pioneered by Dr. Michael Terman of the New York State Psychiatric Institute, dawn simulation mimics the gradually increasing light intensity of the pre-dawn sky. The light output of an incandescent lamp located near your bed is slowly turned up by a computer-programmed electronic device. You can toss and turn or sleep like a baby in the early morning hours with your back turned to the light. It still works.

How can dawn simulation function as a successful antidepressant if your eyes are closed? Try this little experiment. In a lit room, put a hand over your eyes and close them. Then, with your eyes still closed, take your hand away. Do you notice a slight brightening? Your eyelids are not totally opaque. They allow a small amount of light through, especially red light. In fact, almost 10 percent of light at the red end of the spec-

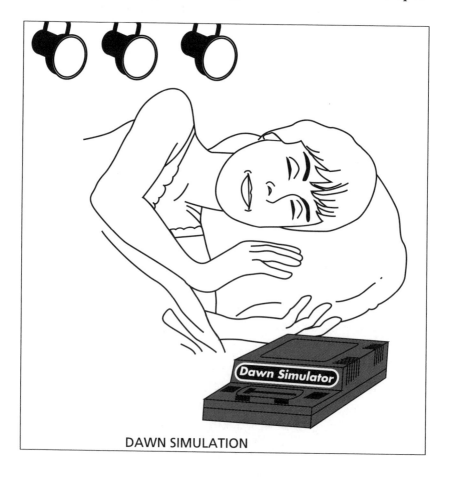

DAWN SIMULATION

trum makes it through your eyelids as opposed to only one to two percent of light in the greens and blues.

The incandescent light used in dawn simulation therapy equipment has a stronger red component than blue or green, so it is particularly efficient at penetrating eyelids. The exceedingly small amount of dim light that does get through falls on the retina at the back of your eyeball — which is most sensitive to light in the early morning hours. Dr. Terman and his colleagues have found this low level of light is sufficient to affect nocturnal sleep patterns. Researchers are on the lookout for other biological mechanisms it could trigger as well.

## Dawn Simulation Trials

In one of several studies proving the effectiveness of dawn simulation, 22 winter SAD patients were told they would receive either a gradual dawn or a rapid dawn simulation while they slept. Unknown to them, the rapid dawn simulation, lasting 30 minutes and reaching a maximum intensity of only 0.2 lux, was a placebo control element. The treatment, which spanned two hours and peaked at 250 lux, proved to be significantly more effective than the control and on par with the results seen in bright light therapy.

Other trials have shown you don't want a dose of dawn therapy much greater than this. Once you exceed a treatment length of two hours or a light peak of 250 lux, some people experience mild to severe early morning awakening. It is also possible to get an overdose of dawn simulation therapy and head into the exaggerated euphoria of Spring Swing.

# Side Effects Of Light Therapy

Most people sail through light therapy without experiencing consequent side effects. However, somewhat less than one in five people who undergo light therapy com-

---

**CLINICALLY SPEAKING**                    **The Placebo Problem**

There is no doubt in anyone's mind. Light therapy works. But how? As you will see in the final chapters of this book, a great deal of research is being done to shed light on this question, but the issue remains cloudy. Some researchers have posed a very different question. Is light therapy nothing more than a highly effective placebo?

In antidepressant medication studies, up to 40 percent of participants from control placebo groups often report improvement in their condition. Similar percentages of light treatment recipients report alleviation of symptoms or complete remission. Are we seeing the placebo effect at work? Or is there true medical advantage to light therapy? And here is an interesting complication. The placebo effect itself is seasonal! In antidepressant medication trials, it has been found that the placebo response is lowest in winter and highest in summer. Does this hold true in light therapy as well?

The major conundrum facing light therapy researchers is the challenge of designing an unambiguous test of light therapy's effectiveness. Such a test would need a control group for comparison — a number of participants who were unknowingly fooled into thinking they were getting light treatment when they were not.

---

plain of **headaches** or **eyestrain**. A number of studies also have noted participants sometimes suffer slight **nausea** in the beginning sessions.

These mild side effects usually go away after the first few days of light therapy. They are neither as severe

---

### The Placebo Problem (cont.)

How do you devise a test of this nature with light? When testing a new drug, the problem doesn't crop up. Trial participants are unable to discern the pill or capsule in question from the placebo used as a control. But participants in light therapy trials cannot help but see the quality and quantity of light they are being treated with and their response to treatment can be influenced at a subconscious level by this knowledge. If a participant believes the treatment he is receiving is the one that works, not the control, he can unconsciously convince himself that his condition is improving, and the placebo effect creeps into the picture. But to what extent? Without a control in the works, it is impossible to know.

Only two light therapy studies to date have incorporated a true placebo device. In the first study, an inactivated negative ion generator was used as the control. Both the control and the 7,000-lux light therapy administered for one hour every morning produced significant reductions in depression scores! In the second study, a low level of negative ions reduced depression scores by only 12% compared to the 60% reduction achieved with 10,000-lux light therapy.

---

nor as long-lasting as the side effects brought about through the use of antidepressant medication, so it is well worth a small amount of temporary discomfort to give light therapy a chance. If the side effects persist, you might be getting an overdose of light. Decrease either the length of your exposure or your proximity to the light unit in small daily increments until the side effects desist.

It is possible to experience an exaggerated response to light therapy, particularly if you are susceptible to episodes of elevated mood in the late spring and in summer. Light therapy fools your brain into thinking the longer days of spring and summer have arrived. Your depression lifts and you go right into the Spring Swing, suddenly experiencing insomnia, irritability or even the recklessness of full-blown mania. If this happens, see your doctor or light therapy clinician immediately. They can provide you with advice as to how you should proceed.

What about the effect of daily exposure to bright artificial lighting on your eyes and skin? We know that excessive exposure to the ultraviolet rays in natural sunshine can lead to the development of cataracts and skin cancer. Might light therapy be equally dangerous?

In short, no. The amount of ultraviolet light given off by the fluorescent bulbs used in light therapy is much lower than the amount of UV you encounter in natural sunlight. The standard light boxes also incorporate the use of a screen between you and the bulbs, which further blocks the emission of ultraviolet light.

Full-spectrum bulbs do, however, have an ultraviolet component comparable to that of natural sunshine and not all of this radiation is screened out by light boxes. Sometimes people with very light complexions find their skin reddens under full-spectrum lights. In this case, a UV-blocking sunscreen lotion can be applied with no subtly harmful result to the light therapy, since light therapy works through the eyes, not the skin.

And what about your eyes? Are they in danger? Dr. Chris Gorman at Foothills Hospital in Calgary has conducted studies in this area and concludes there is no evidence that the fluorescent lights used in light therapy cause damage to the retina at the back of the eye.

It is far more difficult, if not impossible, to gauge the probability of cataract formation due to artificial light exposure. Two unavoidable factors immediately invalidate any attempt to do so. To begin with, most participants in SAD studies are middle-aged. This is the time of life when cataracts normally first show up, regardless of whether or not someone has been undergoing light therapy. How can researchers determine which factor—age or light therapy—has caused any single case of cataract?

The other unavoidable kink in any study regarding UV and cataract formation is the increasing level of UV radiation making its way through the earth's diminishing ozone layer. All light therapy studies to date have taken place within the short time period of the last decade — the same time period that has seen the greatest increase in sunlight UV levels at the earth's surface. People with seasonal affective disorder don't stay indoors all year. When spring arrives, they get out in the sunshine just like anyone else. So how can researchers separate the harmful effects of sunlight from those of artificial light therapy?

# Before You Undertake Light Therapy

Prior to undertaking light therapy, you and your doctor should discuss any occurrence of eye disease in yourself or your family. Following this discussion, your doctor might advise you to have your eyes checked out by an ophthalmologist. An ophthalmologist is qualified to diagnose abnormalities and diseases of the eye and should be able to determine if you have any pre-existing retinal damage that might be made worse by light treatment.

The following "Amsler Grid" will give you a preliminary indication whether you have existing eye problems that need to be checked out before proceeding with light therapy. It is part of the Columbia Eye Check-up for Users of Light Treatment, which is reproduced in full in Appendix F. If your doctor refers you to an ophthalmologist, you may wish to take this along.

It is also important to avoid light therapy if you are taking any medication that sensitizes your eyes to light. In their sensitized state, your eyes might sustain retinal damage when exposed to the extremely bright light used in light therapy.

And one final cautionary note: If you do not suffer from SAD, do not undertake light therapy in an attempt to elevate your mood. **Light therapy does not work on non-SAD people.** In fact, recent research shows the application of light therapy to non-SAD individuals makes them feel worse! They become irritable, anxious and agitated.

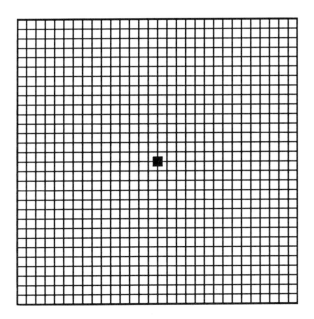

## How to Use the Amsler Grid

If you wear glasses for near vision, be sure to use them for this test. In a well-lit room, hold the chart directly in front of you at arm's length. Place the palm of your free hand over one eye, so it is completely blocked. Look only at the center black dot on the display, while you examine the chart carefully for any perception of wavy lines or blank areas. (If there are no problems, you should see the entire chart as a perfectly aligned piece of graph paper.) Then switch hands, and test the other eye. If you note any distortions in the image, with either or both eyes, you should consult an ophthalmologist before commencing light therapy. *Used with permission of the New York State Psychiatric Institute.*

# CHAPTER 9

# Medications

T HE COMBINED USE OF LIGHT THERAPY and medication can be a powerful weapon in the battle against seasonal affective disorder.

It is true that some medications alone are as effective as light therapy, but by adding light therapy to your routine, you might be able to reduce the amount of medication required. When you consider the possible side effects of many drugs, the opportunity to reduce the dosage is most welcome.

The trick is in finding exactly the correct medication for you. This is determined by a number of different factors, including your general state of health and your receptivity to certain drugs. Don't be discouraged if you begin a round of medication and still do not feel better after several days. Most antidepressant drugs require up to four weeks to take effect.

The information in this chapter is meant to help you understand what the common drugs used in the treatment of SAD are and how they work. It is a simplified version and by no means offers sufficient knowledge for you to self-prescribe drugs. **Undertake a course of medication only in consultation with a qualified healthcare professional.**

# How Drugs Work in Your Brain

All the information that speeds around from one part of your brain to another is handled by specialized nerve cells called "neurons." The neuron is an elongated cell that can receive signals at one end and transmit signals out nerve endings at the other end. But most of the brain activity that is affected by drugs occurs in the infinitesimal gaps between neurons.

There are at least five different chemicals in the human brain that act as messengers across these tiny "synaptic" gaps. They are called "neurotransmitters." Drugs can enhance the message-carrying ability of a specific neurotransmitter in two ways. Drugs can mimic the neurotransmitter and deliver the messages themselves or they can step in and make it easier for the neurotransmitter to do the job. Often this is achieved by preventing ("blocking") the neurotransmitter's inactivation, a neutralizing process that usually happens very quickly after the neurotransmitter is released.

Vast systems of neurons manage different nervous functions of the body. Each system uses a distinct set of neurotransmitters. Two of particular interest in relation to mood are *norepinephrine* and *serotonin*. Norepinephrine is a neurotransmitter found in the neuronal systems of the brain that deal with emotions. These systems, when stimulated, bring about alertness and an overwhelming sense of well-being. Norepinephrine is "turned off" by being reabsorbed back into the very nerve ending that released it. By inhibiting reabsorption of norepinephrine, stimulant drugs such as amphetamines and tricyclic antidepressants extend the euphoric effect of this neurotransmitter.

Norepinephrine also is inactivated when it is broken down by enzymes. So drugs that prevent this enzyme action enhance the presence of norepinephrine and extend a sense of euphoria or well-being. One such enzyme is *monoamine oxidase*. A number of drugs called monoamine oxidase inhibitors (MAOIs) are used as antidepressants.

Serotonin is another neurotransmitter found in the brain that works within the neuronal systems regulating mood. Low levels of serotonin impede the functioning of these neuronal systems and bring about depression. There are now a couple of drugs available for SAD patients that act as antidepressants by inhibiting reabsorption of serotonin in the brain. The much touted Prozac is one. Although relatively expensive compared to tricyclic antidepressants, these serotonin enhancers are proving to cause fewer serious side effects.

# SAD Medications

The following material outlines the general properties of the drugs currently prescribed in the treatment of seasonal affective disorder. Each drug is listed under its pharmaceutical name with the name or names it is marketed under shown in parentheses.

If you would like to learn more about a specific medication, consult your doctor, your pharmacist or one of the many excellent reference books on over-the-counter and prescription drugs available in many bookstores and at most libraries. Also, see "Further Reading" at the back of this book.

## • Tricyclic antidepressants

The fact that tricyclic drugs can be used as antidepressants came as a total surprise when the first of their number, imipramine, was introduced in the 1950s. Imipramine was designed to mimic the chemical structure and function of tranquillizers used in the treatment of schizophrenia. But soon after its antidepressant nature was recognized, it was successfully applied to the treatment of depressive mood disorders.

This extremely effective class of drugs heightens mood by preventing reabsorption of the neurotransmitter norepinephrine. The longer norepinephrine lingers in your brain, the more you benefit from the sense of well-being it induces. If you are depressed, tricyclic drugs relieve your symptoms. If you are not depressed, tricylic drugs act in their original capacity as tranquillizers and sedate you.

**Imipramine** (Tofranil, Tipramine, Janimine) (In Canada: Tofranil, Impril, Novopramine)

*Start-up time:* ten days to six weeks.

*Special requirements:* should be taken on an empty stomach for best effect. If this disturbs your stomach, a small amount of food can be eaten at the same time.

*Advantages:* No dietary restrictions. Fewer side effects than amitriptiline.

*Potential side effects:* weight gain, constipation, difficulty urinating, dry mouth, dizziness from low blood pressure, blurred vision, ringing in the ears, headache, numbness, insomnia, drowsiness, weakness, tremor, confusion, nervousness, excitation, sweating, mania, nausea, skin rashes, photosensitization, irregular heartbeat, high blood pressure (very rare), a drop in blood pressure upon sitting up or standing, change in libido, swollen sex glands, impaired sexual functioning.

*Prohibitions:*

- Do not stop taking this drug suddenly. You may experience headache and nausea as a result.
- Do not take imipramine if you have glaucoma, have a history of seizures, have an enlarged prostate gland or if you have recently suffered a heart attack.
- Do not take barbiturates, epinephrine, norepinephrine, cimetidine or methylphenidate.
- Do not drink alcoholic beverages.
- Wait 14 days after discontinuation of monoamine oxidase inhibitors before starting on imiprimine.

**Desipramine** (Norpramin, Pertofrane) (In Canada: Pertofrane)

*Start-up time:* ten days to six weeks.

*Special requirements:* best when taken on an empty stomach. A small amount of food can be eaten at the same time if the drug alone irritates your stomach.

*Advantages:* no dietary restrictions.

*Potential side effects:* similar but fewer side effects than imipramine.

*Prohibitions:* same as imipramine. Also contraindicated for people with existing kidney or liver disease.

## • Serotonin enhancers

Low levels of the neurotransmitter serotonin in the brain are linked to depression, so drugs that promote increased serotonin levels have an antidepressant effect. Serotonin-active antidepressants may be particularly suited to the treatment of seasonal affective disorder because studies indicate improper regulation of serotonin levels in the brain may be one of the root causes of SAD.

**Fluoxetine** (Prozac)

*Start-up time:* ten days to six weeks.

*Special requirements:* take in the morning or it may interfere with sleep. Nausea can be avoided by taking the medication with your breakfast.

*Advantages:* may be as effective as light therapy in the treatment of seasonal affective disorder. Less toxic than tricyclic antidepressants. No dietary restrictions.

*Potential side effects:* upper respiratory distress and infection (similar to a cold or flu), chills, flushing, skin rashes, headache, dizziness, drowsiness, unusual dreams, insomnia, anxiety, nervousness, tremor, ringing in the ears, jaw or muscle pain, weakness, palpitations, slow or irregular heartbeat, dry mouth, painful menstruation, sexual dysfunction, urinary tract infection, gastrointestinal problems (nausea, vomiting, heartburn, gas, constipation, diarrhea) with attendant weight loss, also increased appetite or water retention with attendant weight gain.

*Prohibitions:*

- Do not take in conjunction with tryptophan, warfarin, digitoxin or MAOIs.
- Do not drink alcoholic beverages.

**Sertraline** (Zoloft)

*Start-up time:* ten days to six weeks.

*Special requirements:* same as Prozac. Best result when taken with food.

*Advantages:* may have less potential to cause anxiety than Prozac. Zoloft also requires less time to clear from your system than Prozac.

## Case Study: PAULA

**"If you see a hint of hope anywhere, go for it,"** advises Paula, a 47-year-old SAD sufferer from Nova Scotia. That's exactly what she did.

For years Paula had been getting off to work every day, functioning only minimally at her job during the winter. "I work independently in my position, so I could shut myself up in my office and not do anything on really bad days," she confesses. "I was a total recluse once I got home. I had no social life because I was physically exhausted and refused to participate in anything. It seems I just cried, slept and ate the entire time I wasn't at work."

Paula's family doctor was unable to help her. Then one day she answered a newspaper ad soliciting participants for a clinical trial of Prozac. "I figured, what do I have to lose? Even if it were to turn out this drug has life-shortening effects, I'd rather live 10 happy years than 30 miserable years."

Much to Paula's delight and relief, Prozac did the trick. "If you have any inkling you have SAD, seek out help. It's there. Don't take 'no' for an answer from your doctor," she urges.

*Potential side effects:* similar to Prozac.

*Prohibitions:* same as Prozac.

**Paroxetine** (Paxil)

*Start-up time:* ten days to six weeks.

*Special requirements:* same as Prozac.

*Advantages:* same as Zoloft.

*Potential side effects:* nausea, somnolence, sweating, tremor, weakness, dizziness, dry mouth, insomnia, male sexual dysfunction, headache, constipation, diarrhea, malaise, high blood pressure, fainting, racing heartbeat, itching, weight gain, weight loss, impaired concentration, depression, vertigo.

*Prohibitions:* same as Prozac.

**Trazodone** (Desyrel)

*Start-up time:* ten days to six weeks.

*Special requirements:* must be taken after meals.

*Advantages:* No dietary restrictions.

*Potential side effects:* stomach upset and loss of appetite, also increased appetite and weight gain, headache,

## Case Study: LOUISE

Louise was diagnosed with SAD a few years ago. Her doctor tried to get her into the local SAD clinic light therapy trial, but it was already underway and could not accommodate Louise. As an alternative treatment, Louise's doctor put her on Prozac. Louise has found the Prozac is quite effective. She's able to keep going during the winter months, holds down a regular job, but still feels she's dragging along from time to time just waiting for long sunny days to arrive.

lack of concentration, impaired memory, agitation, anxiety, nervousness, insomnia, nightmares, anger, constipation, increased urination, dry mouth, ringing in the ears, confusion, fatigue, drowsiness, weakness, fuzzy vision, dizziness, tremors, sudden drop in blood pressure upon sitting up or standing, skin rashes, sweating, sexual dysfunction, decreased sex drive (males), increased sex drive (females), irregular menstruation (rare) and, very rarely, priapism (a painful erection that requires medical attention).

*Prohibitions:*

- Do not take in combination with alcoholic beverages, digoxin, phenytoin, or blood pressure medication.
- Do not use if you are recovering from a heart attack or undergoing electroshock therapy.

## • Monoamine Oxidase Inhibitors (MAOIs)

This is another class of drugs that was initially developed to treat something quite different than depression. The first monoamine oxidase inhibitor, iproniazid (which has since been withdrawn), surprised the medical community when it improved the moods of depressed tuberculosis patients to whom it was administered to a greater extent than it cleared up their infections, the drug's initial objective.

MAOIs increase the levels of neurotransmitters in the brain by preventing their enzymatic breakdown. They are particularly effective in the case of individuals experiencing weight gain, increased appetite and hypersomnia, the symptoms seen so often in seasonal affective disorder. However, when on MAOIs, there is the ever-present potential to develop a sudden, dangerous increase in blood pressure if foods containing tyramine are ingested. For this reason, MAOIs are usually prescribed only if tricyclic or serotonin-enhancing antidepressants prove ineffective or are contraindicated (made inadvisable).

**Phenelzine** (Nardil)

*Start-up time:* ten days to six weeks.

*Special requirements:* observe dietary restrictions (see prohibitions) for no less than ten days following discontinuation of medication. Take early in the day to avoid sleep disturbance. If you are on diabetic medication, your dosage may have to be altered.

*Advantages:* effective alternate when tricyclic antidepressants and serotonin enhancers fail or are contraindicated.

*Potential side effects:* liver dysfunction, sexual dysfunction, decreased sex drive, nausea, sweating, constipation, loss of appetite, dry mouth, fatigue, drowsiness, dizziness, confusion, mania, muscle twitching, tremors, excitation, memory impairment, irregular heartbeat, high blood pressure, sudden drop in blood pressure upon standing or sitting up, skin rash, urine retention, swelling, sleep disturbances, weight gain, blurred vision, glaucoma.

*Prohibitions:*
- Not to be taken by anyone with liver dysfunction, congestive heart failure, heart or cerebrovascular disease, high blood pressure; by anyone who suffers migraine or frequent headaches; or by the elderly.

- Consult your doctor or pharmacist regarding which drugs cannot be taken with Nardil but, as a general guideline, do not take in combination with levodopa, amphetamines, cocaine, antihistamines, ephedrine, pethidine (meperidine in the U.S.), metaraminol, methotrimeprazine, methylphenidate, phenyl-ephrine, phenylpropanolamine, sedatives, tricyclic antidepressants, narcotics, alcohol (not even alcohol-free or reduced-alcohol beer or wine products) or cold and allergy medicine containing dextro-methorphan.
- Do not use within ten days of surgery or local anesthetic.
- Do not eat cheese, yogurt, sour cream, broad beans, pickled fish, beef or chicken liver, red wine, marinated meat, any partly spoiled foods or meat and yeast extracts (Bovril, Oxo, etc.), or excessive amounts of chocolate or caffeine.
- Do not use within 5 weeks of discontinuing fluoxetine (Prozac).

**Tranylcypromine Sulfate** (Parnate, Transamine Sulfate)

*Start-up time:* two to four weeks.

*Special requirements:* observe dietary restrictions (see prohibitions) for no less than ten days following discontinuation of medication. Take early in the day to avoid sleep disturbance. If you are on diabetic medication, your dosage may have to be altered. The use of anti-Parkinsonian medications or spinal anesthetics in conjunction with this drug should be monitored closely by your physician.

*Advantages:* effective alternate when tricyclic anti-depressants and serotonin enhancers fail or are contraindicated.

*Potential side effects:* sexual dysfunction, altered sex drive, headache, insomnia, drowsiness, nausea, urinary retention, sweating, chills, constipation, diarrhea, loss of appetite, dry mouth, fatigue, dizziness, vertigo, blurred vision, confusion, mania, muscle twitching, tremors, excitation, memory impairment, irregular heartbeat, high blood pressure, sudden drop in blood pressure upon standing or sitting up, skin rash, swelling.

*Prohibitions:*

- Not to be taken by anyone with liver or kidney dysfunction, congestive heart failure, heart or cerebrovascular disease, pheochromocytoma, high blood pressure, by anyone who is on diuretics, who suffers migraine or frequent headaches, or who is elderly, feeble or suicidal.
- Do not take in combination with levodopa, dibenzazepine derivatives, amphetamines, antihistamines, ephedrine, pethidine (meperidine in the U.S.), metaraminol, methotrimeprazine, methylphenidate, phenylephrine, phenylpropanolamine, sedatives, tricyclic antidepressants, narcotics, alcohol or cold and allergy medicine containing dextromethorphan.
- Do not use within seven days of surgery or local anesthetic.
- Do not eat cheese, yogurt, sour cream, broad beans, pickled fish, beef or chicken liver, red wine, marinated meat, any partly spoiled foods or meat and yeast extracts (Bovril, Oxo, etc.).

- **Bupropion hydrochloride** (Wellbutrin)
  (Not available in Canada)

Neither a tricyclic antidepressant nor a monoamine oxidase inhibitor, the relatively new antidepressant bupropion affects levels of the neurotransmitters norepinephrine, dopamine and serotonin. In one recent study headed by Dr. S.C. Dilsaver, two-thirds of SAD patients given bupropion showed outstanding improvement and the remainder responded positively but to a lesser degree. The primary drawback to use of bupropion is the potential for suffering seizures.

*Start-up time:* up to several weeks.

*Special requirements:* use with caution if you are taking levodopa. Check with your physician or pharmacist before using in conjunction with any other prescription or over-the-counter medication. While taking bupropion, if you are on benzodiazepines and need to withdraw, do so gradually.

*Advantages:* relatively few anticholinergic or cardiovascular side effects and minimal, if any, drowsiness. No dietary restrictions. More likely to promote weight loss than weight gain — a boon for people who have winter SAD.

*Potential side effects:* seizures, symptoms similar to flu, dry and/or sore mouth, sleep impairment, sedation, irregular heartbeat, palpitations, abnormal blood pressure, arthritis, confusion, lack of co-ordination, tremor, faintness, headache, ear problems, water retention or frequent urination, constipation, heartburn, nausea, blurred vision, menstrual problems, sexual dysfunction, irritability, euphoria, delusions and anxiety.

*Prohibitions:*
- Do not take bupropion if you have taken MAOIs within the prior two weeks, if you are nursing a baby, if you have a seizure disorder, or if in the past you have suffered head trauma or have been prone to tumors of the central nervous system or eating disorders.
- Do not take in conjunction with tricyclic antidepressants, MAOIs, phenothiazines or phenobarbital.

- **Lithium Carbonate** (Eskalith, Lithane, Lithobid, Lithonate, Lithotabs, Cibalith-S) (In Canada: Carbolith, Lithane, Lithizine)

Although lithium carbonate has been in use since 1949, it is still unknown exactly how this drug does what it does. It was initially used to battle "cluster" headaches and to forestall relapses of manic episodes in psychiatric patients. Current research has shown lithium to be effective against seasonal affective disorder. In one study, nearly 60 percent of SAD patients diagnosed as manic-depressive and treated with lithium carbonate experienced complete or nearly complete remission of their symptoms. The result was even more impressive when lithium was given to SAD patients with recurrent depression. Over 70 percent showed a marked decrease in the severity of their symptoms.

In spite of these encouraging results, lithium carbonate is usually reserved for patients with Manic Depressive illness. It has some truly frightening potential side effects, which include seizures, blackouts and coma. Just a few of its less severe side effects are headache, dizziness, low blood pressure, lowered white blood cell count, lack of co-ordination, a metallic taste in the mouth, vomiting, diarrhea, skin rashes, incontinence, thinning hair and impotence.

If you are on lithium carbonate, it is important to be careful when using sodium chloride (salt), sodium bi-carbonate (baking soda and baking powder) and aminophylline. These substances might diminish the beneficial effects of lithium. Conversely, the use of diuretics can lead to retention of lithium in your system. Lithium can become toxic if taken in combination with the drugs methyldopa, carbamazepine, indomethacin, probenecid or piroxicam and can cause brain syndrome if taken with haloperidol or thioridazine.

Lithium carbonate generally requires one to three weeks to take effect. It is important to keep your fluid intake up while you are on this medication. Down it with an ample glass of water after meals.

# CHAPTER 10

# Psychotherapy

**I**T IS QUITE COMMON FOR PEOPLE WITH seasonal affective disorder to seek out professional help from a counsellor or psychotherapist at some point in their lives, especially when the going gets particularly rough, say following the death of a loved one or the break-up of a marriage. It is difficult enough dealing with the depression of SAD, let alone trying to jump emotional hurdles anyone would find challenging. Psychotherapy can be extremely helpful at these times.

Beyond crisis situations, psychotherapy can also serve as an effective means of dealing with some of the self-destructive mindsets people with seasonal affective disorder are prone to adopt. Can professional

## Case Study: DAVINA

Davina — a teacher of many years, now approaching retirement — says she's been bothered with fatigue, the blues and altered sleep patterns beginning early every November for as long as she can remember. Seven years ago, she started falling into clinical depressions and was put on antidepressant medication. Three years ago, Davina lost one of her daughters to cystic fibrosis. Thereafter, when depression settled in, "it was difficult to know whether it was due to grief or SAD," says Davina.

counselling help in your case? Here are a few samples of the type of mental state you might be experiencing which would benefit from psychotherapy.

# The Endless Loop

You are in a mental rut. Somehow, no matter how sincere you are in your efforts to break the pattern, you just go right on making the same mistakes time after time. The way out of your "endless loop," to use computer lingo, is not at all obvious from where you stand. But a trained psychotherapist can be quite good at spotting the EXIT sign and pointing you in that direction.

# The Downward Spiral of Self-Esteem

For years now, you have repeatedly lost jobs and, perhaps, relationships as a result of SAD, but you don't quite see it that way. Instead you blame yourself for being a failure. Your self-esteem plummets, resulting in even less ability to cope, more failures, further loss of self-esteem, less coping ability, more failures, more loss of self-esteem . . . a vicious spiral with the destructive force of a tornado. This way of thinking can be extremely harmful to your well-being. A psychotherapist can do two things for you. The first problem that needs to be addressed is your SAD-related depression. Once this is under control, any residual feelings of low self-esteem can be tackled.

There are many different types of therapist you could consult, depending on the type of problems you are

## Case Study: CARLA's Coping Tip

Carla (see Chapter 5 ) was at first reluctant to go into cognitive therapy. "It was too 'touchy-feely' for me," she recounts. "But its effect really kicked in when I seriously committed myself to it. **I have an entire page of positive thoughts committed to memory.** When I begin to feel down, I recite my way through the material. This has proven remarkably successful in lifting my mood."

encountering: cognitive therapists, behavioral therapists, psychoanalysts. In many cases, it is impossible to recognize the nature of your own problem. How do you decide which type of therapy is best? Your family physician can help you. He or she has likely seen you over several years and knows the extent of your SAD-related symptoms, including depression. This is someone you trust and, when informed regarding the mental bugbears that are bothering you, someone who should be able to refer you to the appropriate therapist.

## Case Study: SUSAN

Susan's blues are a near regular occurrence every winter. During these times she tries to maintain a positive outlook by reminding herself she's actually a very capable person. "I just concentrate on the fact **I can handle anything when the sun shines.**"

# CHAPTER 11

# Exercise and Diet

**P**EOPLE WHO SUFFER THE DEPRESSION and fatigue of the winter blues and full-blown SAD can find it difficult to get out of bed, let alone make it through the list of tasks that must be done at the office or around the house. Often the energy — both physical and mental — required to prepare meals just isn't there. Fast, convenient, high-fat, high-carbohydrate foods end up forming the basis of SAD meals and the pounds pile on. What can you do? The mere mention of exercise seems ludicrous.

Don't despair! In this chapter you will learn how to make food work for you, instead of against you. You'll also see how to take advantage of the fact your depression is seasonal to establish lifestyle routines that will take you through the rough times on "automatic pilot."

## Exercise

On a nice day, modern urbanites spend, on average, about one and a half hours outdoors. Statistics regarding the number of hours spent outside during the short daylight period of freezing winter days are not available at present, but it's probably safe to assume the number drops off drastically. It is not at all unusual to drive to work in the pre-dawn dark, eat lunch at the office and leave for home just in time to wave goodnight to the sun as its feeble rays fade on the southwestern horizon. Blah!

If you are clinically SAD, getting up enough energy and motivation to undertake outdoor physical activity during the inclement winter months can be an immense challenge. But keep reminding yourself, the more hours you spend out in the sunshine, the better you are going to feel. Start out slowly. Perhaps two or three 15-minute spells outdoors might be all you are able to muster at first. Don't even think about vigorous exercise at this point. Just try to stay in the sunshine and keep moving, if for no other reason than simply to stay warm!

*Note: The best strategy is to begin an exercise routine* **before** *your symptoms show up. An established pattern is easier to stick with. Many people also find they are more motivated to persist in their efforts to exercise if they have an exercise partner who provides psychological support and urges them on.*

As the weeks go by, you should begin to feel more energetic and less inclined to hide away at home. Why? Because 30 minutes outdoors, even on an overcast fall or winter day, will expose you to the same amount of light as spending 30 minutes in front of a 10,000-lux light box, a dose found highly effective against the symptoms of SAD.

Those of you with winter blues can begin with a more aggressive approach to exercise. Brisk strolls around the block on your lunch break, ice-skating and cross-country skiing on weekends, all can help put you in a sunnier mood. Not only will you be exposed to more sunlight, but the exercise should help keep your weight in check and improve your sleep problems.

If you are confined indoors, don't pass up the benefits of exercise just because it is not being done in the sunshine. Exercise, especially aerobic exercise, can go a long way toward putting you in a better frame of mind. Is there a staircase in your home or office building you can walk up and down? If this sounds too strenuous, try mall walking. Just keep moving!

Important things happen when you perform vigorous physical activity. Your heart muscle gets exercise and over time, becomes more efficient at its job of pumping oxygenated blood to all parts of your body. At the cellular level, oxygen breaks down the nutrients in the food you eat and so creates more energy for you to expend. Increased circulation of blood to your limbs and joints also helps overcome stiffness and aching that sometimes shows up in seasonal affective disorder. And here is a real boon for people with the blues — exercise, especially when done outside, can go a long way toward relieving stress and improving your mood. In fact, one study has shown that, if you jog outdoors for half an hour at least three times per week, your depression will lift as effectively as if you had seen a psychotherapist instead.

What about wearing sunglasses when you exercise outdoors? Do they cut down on the amount of light reaching your eyes to the extent that wearing them contributes to SAD? As yet, this question has not been addressed by the research community.

We do know that prolonged exposure to the ultra-violet component of natural sunlight ultimately results in damage to the eyes and sunglasses are beneficial in preventing this from happening.

Perhaps the solution for people with SAD lies in a newly-developed eyeglass filter that completely eliminates UV light while maximizing transmission of visible light. See Appendix E for the supplier of this technological breakthrough.

# Food and Mood

Why do all those carbohydrate-rich, sweet and fattening foods hold such irresistible appeal? Why don't you stop eating when everyone else at the table has had their fill? Why do you continue munching down the potato chips, nibbling on the pasta leftovers or binging on cheesecake even though you realize your clothes are getting snugger every day?

As explained in Chapter 2, these behavioral patterns are a totally unconscious attempt on your part to raise your spirits. The consumption of food high in carbohydrate content brings about elevation of serotonin levels in your brain — and this makes you feel better. Pure and simple.

Or is it? You should reach a point during your meal when this beneficial effect of carbohydrate consumption kicks in and you feel sated. But for many SAD people this doesn't happen. Their appetite actually grows the more they eat carbohydrates. What's going on?

When you ingest carbohydrates, a chain of events is set off that normally ends in the production of serotonin. In your digestive system, the food energy that carbohydrates provide is transformed into the blood sugar "glucose." Within minutes, insulin (a hormone produced in the pancreas) is released into your bloodstream. Insulin is responsible for transporting the glucose where it is required throughout the body. As delivery of the glucose is completed, the insulin in your bloodstream drops below a certain level. This cue triggers production of serotonin in the brain and you get the message that all is well and you can stop eating.

The amount of insulin released to deal with the meal is at the root of the overeaters' problem. The body normally does a self-check and releases just the right amount of insulin based on how much was required in previous meals. For overeaters, this feedback mechanism goes awry. The amount of insulin released during a meal is out of all proportion to the amount actually needed. The insulin level in the blood remains high and

## Case Study: CARLA's Conundrum

Carla figures she would not weigh 350 pounds today if she had not suffered from SAD all her life. **"I can remember sneaking food as early as nine or ten years of age.** I was chunky and very tall even then."

"It's been a vicious catch-22 all the way," says Carla. "When I'm depressed, I eat. Then I get even more depressed when I gain weight."

the brain doesn't receive the signal to generate serotonin. The brain interprets this abundance of insulin as hunger and the overeater goes right on eating, causing the body to produce even more insulin in the process!

Fortunately, light therapy is highly effective for individuals who struggle with this symptom of SAD. Many light therapy recipients report a decrease in appetite and carbohydrate craving after only a few days of treatment.

As an adjunct to light therapy, you can strategize your eating behavior to minimize weight gain and maximize the self-medicating aspect of food consumption. You might even wish to use diet as an alternative to light therapy if you fall into the seasonally blue category and find low mood does not present as great a problem as increased appetite. What you eat and when you eat it are critical.

# What to Eat

Let's first analyze the type of food you should eat, regardless of whether you wish to maintain your current weight or take off pounds you have recently acquired. You crave carbohydrate-rich foods, but carbohydrates come in two different forms that are absorbed into your body at different rates.

"Simple" carbohydrates are the sugars you encounter in sweets. They are absorbed quickly and supply the kind of energy boost you get as soon as you eat a candy bar. The problem is, you ingest a considerable amount of carbohydrate for a fleeting effect. The old adage "A moment on the lips, a lifetime on the hips" is exactly what we are talking about. Wouldn't it be better if you could make that same amount of carbohydrate intake work for you over an extended period of time — get more bang for your buck, so to speak?

Well, you can. The other form of carbohydrate, often referred to as "complex" carbohydrate, is absorbed far more slowly than simple carbohydrate. We're talking potatoes, pasta, oatmeal, rice, bread — all those wonderful comfort foods. If you have a meal that includes one or more of these sources of complex carbohydrate, your body will gradually absorb them over the next several hours, keeping your serotonin levels up the entire time. You should experience a reprieve from that compelling urge to snack between meals. If this effect wears off before your next regular meal and you just have to have something to tide you over, remember this: it takes only 1.5 ounces (4 grams) of carbohydrate to kick start the serotonin generator in your brain again. So try not to eat more than is necessary to do the job.

Most SAD people crave carbohydrates due to the self-medicating effect they provide, but not all SAD people react to a carbohydrate-laden meal the same way. If you are like most SAD carbohydrate cravers, in the hour or so after eating one of these meals you feel more energized, less depressed and more able to concentrate on the things you have to get done. There are some SAD people, however, who

> **1.5 Ounces of Carbohydrate Equals:**
>
> - 2 celery stalks
>   or
> - ½ cookie
>   or
> - ⅓ orange
>   or
> - ¼ apple
>   or
> - ½ tsp. raisins

feel sluggish and less alert after such a meal. These people likely find a protein-rich meal energizes them in much the same way a carbohydrate-laden meal energizes most SAD people.

The secret to maximizing your energy level and improving your mood lies in determining exactly how *you* react to carbohydrates and proteins. Remember, if you increase your energy level, you will feel more inclined to exercise. And more exercise, in turn, improves your spirits and leads to an overall *decrease* in appetite. You win all around!

Here is how to go about determining which type of nutrient — protein or carbohydrate — works most beneficially for you. Over a four-day period, ensure that each meal you eat is made up primarily of protein the first two days and primarily of carbohydrate the next two days. Don't combine high-protein and high-carbohydrate food in the same meal. You can use the meal planning suggestions and recipes supplied in Appendix B or make up your own meals using the following categories as a guide. Avoid the foods that contain both protein and carbohydrate as they will confuse the results of the trial.

- **Foods High in Protein:**
  beef, pork, lamb, chicken, fish, eggs, cheese, hot dog, tofu.
- **Foods High in Carbohydrates:**
  potato, pasta, rice, cereal, bread, crackers, fruit-flavored yogurt, fruit; fresh and canned corn, peas, squash, turnip, beets and fruit juice; regular soft drinks, pancakes, waffles, ice cream, sherbet, pie,

cake, cookies, chocolate, candy (lifesavers, lollipops, mints, etc.), syrup, jams, jelly, honey, popcorn.
- **Foods Containing both Protein and Carbohydrate:** milk, plain or diet yogurt, peanut butter, nuts, beans, kidney beans, lentils, baked beans.

During this four-day trial, do not drink beverages that might alter your mood. They will muddy the results. These include wine, spirits and any beverages containing caffeine — such as coffee, tea or soft drinks. Decaffeinated coffee and soft drinks, herbal tea and water are fine. Also note the results of this trial might be confused if you carry it out during a four-day period when you are encountering unusual levels of stress. If this is the case, you will want to wait a while and try it at another time.

On the accompanying chart, carefully record how you feel immediately before each meal and how you feel approximately one hour after the meal. Also confine snacking to the time interval between your post-meal assessment and the point one hour before your next meal.

Now look at your filled-in chart and see if you can find a pattern. Note whether or not you show a decided tendency to feel calmer, more energized and more alert after carbohydrate meals or protein meals. This information will help you determine the type of food that should form the basis of your winter meal-planning strategy.

**Type of meal** — (check off applicable box or boxes)

| | Pre-meal mood | | | | | | | | | | | | | | | | | | Post-meal mood | | | | | | | | | | | | | | | | | |
|---|---|---|---|---|---|---|---|---|---|---|---|---|---|---|---|---|---|---|---|---|---|---|---|---|---|---|---|---|---|---|---|---|---|---|---|---|
| | Calm | | | Agitated | | | Tired | | | Energized | | | Depressed | | | Alert | | | Calm | | | Agitated | | | Tired | | | Energized | | | Depressed | | | Alert | | |
| **Day 1** | | | | | | | | | | | | | | | | | | | | | | | | | | | | | | | | | | | | |
| Breakfast (protein) | ☐ | ☐ | ☐ | ☐ | ☐ | ☐ | ☐ | ☐ | ☐ | ☐ | ☐ | ☐ | ☐ | ☐ | ☐ | ☐ | ☐ | ☐ | ☐ | ☐ | ☐ | ☐ | ☐ | ☐ | ☐ | ☐ | ☐ | ☐ | ☐ | ☐ | ☐ | ☐ | ☐ | ☐ | ☐ | ☐ |
| Lunch (protein) | | | | | | | | | | | | | | | | | | | | | | | | | | | | | | | | | | | | |
| Dinner (protein) | | | | | | | | | | | | | | | | | | | | | | | | | | | | | | | | | | | | |
| **Day 2** | | | | | | | | | | | | | | | | | | | | | | | | | | | | | | | | | | | | |
| Breakfast (protein) | ☐ | ☐ | ☐ | ☐ | ☐ | ☐ | ☐ | ☐ | ☐ | ☐ | ☐ | ☐ | ☐ | ☐ | ☐ | ☐ | ☐ | ☐ | ☐ | ☐ | ☐ | ☐ | ☐ | ☐ | ☐ | ☐ | ☐ | ☐ | ☐ | ☐ | ☐ | ☐ | ☐ | ☐ | ☐ | ☐ |
| Lunch (protein) | | | | | | | | | | | | | | | | | | | | | | | | | | | | | | | | | | | | |
| Dinner (protein) | | | | | | | | | | | | | | | | | | | | | | | | | | | | | | | | | | | | |
| **Day 3** | | | | | | | | | | | | | | | | | | | | | | | | | | | | | | | | | | | | |
| Breakfast (carbohydrate) | ☐ | ☐ | ☐ | ☐ | ☐ | ☐ | ☐ | ☐ | ☐ | ☐ | ☐ | ☐ | ☐ | ☐ | ☐ | ☐ | ☐ | ☐ | ☐ | ☐ | ☐ | ☐ | ☐ | ☐ | ☐ | ☐ | ☐ | ☐ | ☐ | ☐ | ☐ | ☐ | ☐ | ☐ | ☐ | ☐ |
| Lunch (carbohydrate) | | | | | | | | | | | | | | | | | | | | | | | | | | | | | | | | | | | | |
| Dinner (carbohydrate) | | | | | | | | | | | | | | | | | | | | | | | | | | | | | | | | | | | | |
| **Day 4** | | | | | | | | | | | | | | | | | | | | | | | | | | | | | | | | | | | | |
| Breakfast (carbohydrate) | ☐ | ☐ | ☐ | ☐ | ☐ | ☐ | ☐ | ☐ | ☐ | ☐ | ☐ | ☐ | ☐ | ☐ | ☐ | ☐ | ☐ | ☐ | ☐ | ☐ | ☐ | ☐ | ☐ | ☐ | ☐ | ☐ | ☐ | ☐ | ☐ | ☐ | ☐ | ☐ | ☐ | ☐ | ☐ | ☐ |
| Lunch (carbohydrate) | | | | | | | | | | | | | | | | | | | | | | | | | | | | | | | | | | | | |
| Dinner (carbohydrate) | | | | | | | | | | | | | | | | | | | | | | | | | | | | | | | | | | | | |

138

# When to Eat

You now know what type of nutrient works best for you, protein or carbohydrate. (A well-balanced diet includes both.) It is simply a matter of determining when to eat each of them to gain the most benefit from their sedating or energizing effects.

If you feel more alert and energized after eating a carbohydrate-rich meal, eat this type of meal before the part of the day when you need to be at your best. For most people this will mean eating a carbohydrate-packed breakfast and lunch to see them through the work day. In the evening, when you want to slow down in preparation for a good night's sleep, have your protein-laden meal for dinner, sit down and relax.

Exactly the opposite routine should work for those of you who pep up with protein. Breakfast and lunch should be strong on lean meat, fish, poultry, eggs and cheese (tofu if you are a vegan) and dinner should be planned around a main course of carbohydrate.

*Note: "Carbohydrate-rich" meals should contain a small amount of protein and "protein-rich" meals should include a small portion of carbohydrate. Total exclusion of one nutrient in favor of the other is a routine that should be followed only during the four-day test period.*

# Minimizing Weight Gain

If you are SAD or blue, one of the best coping strategies you can adopt is the practice of setting realistic goals. This applies especially well to the issue of weight gain. When your SAD symptoms are at their worst, consider yourself successful if you simply keep weight gain to a minimum.

Here are some tips that should help you avoid putting on the pounds.

- **Eat regular meals.**

This enables blood sugars to remain more constant throughout the day, so your body doesn't make too much insulin. An overabundance of insulin can cause dietary calories to be turned into fat which settles on the upper body. Get on a regular meal schedule when you have lots of energy and this habitual eating pattern should carry you through your SAD period.

- **Avoid high-fat foods or fatty cooking methods, such as deep fat frying.**

Fat is the most concentrated source of calories. Minimizing the use of fat can help you maintain or even lose weight. If you reduce fat intake by two teaspoons per day, you can achieve weight loss of about 10 pounds in one year (assuming your exercise routine and remaining nutrient intake remain constant).

Many people turn to fast food outlets when their energy levels are too low to prepare a meal at home. This strategy is fine on occasion, but compare the fat content of fast foods (see **Fat in Fast Foods**) to the fat in a single portion of a few of the quick and easy recipes provided in Appendix B (indicated by *).

- **Choose a variety of high-fiber foods.**

These include whole grain breads, cereals, fresh fruits, vegetables and pulses (dried peas, beans and lentils). Research indicates calories eaten along with fiber cause less weight gain. Fiber also is useful because it can draw water into the intestine from surrounding

| Fat in Fast Foods | Calories | Grams of Fat |
|---|---|---|
| Hamburger with cheese | 500 | 30 |
| Pepperoni pizza (individual size) | 530 | 21 |
| Beef enchilada | 315 | 15 |
| Chicken nuggets (6) | 276 | 18 |
| Fish (2 pieces) and fries | 853 | 48 |
| Easy Oven Beef and Vegetable Stew* | 235 | 5 |
| Family Favorite Shepherd's Pie* | 324 | 12 |
| Bev's Best Stir Fry* | 203 | 8 |
| Bean and Pasta Soup* (1 ½ c.) | 130 | 3 |

cells. It is thought this helps you feel full while your food is digesting.

- **Drink adequate fluid to keep your body hydrated (six to eight 8-ounce glasses per day).**

If fluid intake is inadequate, the kidneys stop working to capacity. The liver drops what it's doing — among other things, metabolizing stored fat into energy — in order to step in and help out. Too little fluid intake also can lead to water retention and constipation and may increase the effect of medications you are taking.

- **Avoid extreme diets.**

The act of going on a diet is one of the best predictors of weight gain. The newest diet advertised as quick and easy on the magazine cover may be tempting but counterproductive in the long run.

Be particularly cautious of high-protein diets which severely restrict carbohydrate intake. Research has shown this type of diet increases the workload of the kidneys to unhealthy levels and, in addition, eventually results in serious carbohydrate craving. You end up back at square one!

- **When you have adequate energy, exercise regularly.**

This may vary from walking around inside your house in mid-winter to participating in tennis or baseball during the summer. Active living plays a role in weight control. It also can help control appetite.

## Avoid the trap of self-reproach

If you give light treatment and weight maintenance your best shot and appetite continues to be a problem, don't let the fact get you down. Absolutely refuse to let something beyond your control dictate how you feel about yourself.

Your best bet is to continue self-medicating with food and accept the fact your wardrobe will have to accommodate the resulting weight gain. Above all else, you shouldn't feel guilty or in any way inadequate because you are gaining weight. You are afflicted with a physiological condition that will eventually abate once the season is over. Self-recrimination will only fuel your sense of depression and make the problem worse.

# Coping with Cooking

You are absolutely famished — dying to sink your teeth into something substantial. But plan and prepare a nutritious meal? Forget it! You are far too depressed and fatigued. What do you do?

Organization and advance preparation are the keys to coping with cooking during the SAD season.

• When you have adequate energy, prepare recipes in bulk and freeze. This can save both preparation and clean-up time later.

---

**Freezing Tips**

To obtain high-quality products:

• shorten regular cooking time by 10 to 20 minutes on recipes to be frozen.

• chill your food well before freezing. This will minimize condensation.

• freeze in one-meal portions. Faster freezing gives better quality.

• freeze in air-tight containers — freezer paper, heavy-duty aluminum foil or plastic freezer bags are the best choice.

• allow ½" to 1" headspace for expansion during freezing.

• date all products you put in the freezer. It is generally recommended frozen products be used within 3 months.

**Thawing and reheating**

• To obtain the best quality, reheat foods without thawing. Unwrap frozen casserole and bake, covered, for 1½ to 2 hours at 325°F for 6 servings or 1¼ hours for 3 servings.

*Courtesy of Canadian Western Natural Gas*
*Blue Flame Kitchen*

---

• Test recipes during the summer to ensure you know the procedure and enjoy the recipe. Several easy-to-prepare, nutritious recipes you may wish to try are provided in Appendix B. Note any shortcuts you have learned on the recipe and cross out any ingredients you don't deem necessary. If concentration is a problem during the SAD season, set out all your ingredients before you begin preparing the recipe, then put each bag, bottle — what have you — away immediately after you add the ingredient to keep track of what has gone in.

---

**Foods that don't freeze well**

• Potatoes become spongy when frozen. They may maintain good quality if cut into small pieces in a soup or stew.

• Strong-flavored vegetables — such as cabbage, turnip and brussel sprouts — don't freeze well.

• Freezing can change the flavor of herbs and spices. Some — onion for example — decrease in flavor when frozen. Spices such as cloves, pimento or pepper may get stronger. Curry can develop a musty flavor. You may need to correct flavoring while reheating.

• Sauces thickened with wheat flour tend to separate on freezing. Canned cream soups or sauces thickened with cornstarch or rice flour freeze well.

• Sauces with a high quantity of milk or cheese will curdle on reheating. They will still taste good, but may not look as appetizing.

*Courtesy of Canadian Western Natural Gas*
*Blue Flame Kitchen*

• Use your crock pot to prepare a soup or stew. This can be a healthy dinner with the added bonus of minimum clean-up afterwards. Cut meat into bite-sized pieces. Canned tomatoes, chicken or beef broth can form the base. A variety of frozen vegetables can be added. Pasta, rice or barley contribute the thickening. Spice as you like.

• If you gather the energy to prepare a meal, cook a large portion so you have leftovers to heat the next day. Most people comment that stews and chilis taste better reheated the second day.

• Organize a large shopping order for all staples while you have energy. Make sure your core recipes can be prepared from the staples at hand. Note any convenience foods in the store which may be purchased and used when your energy is low. For example, there are low-fat frozen dinners available that microwave in just a few minutes.

• Delegate tasks to other family members whenever possible. You might even keep a cache of canned or frozen foods they feel capable of preparing on days when you're not up to setting foot in the kitchen.

• Test the quality and ingredients in nearby take-out restaurants before winter sets in. Some people are lucky enough to have a great deli close to their office or on their route home.

• Make simple menu plans ahead of time to simplify meal preparation or to give the family a framework in which they can offer some help.

# CHAPTER 12

# Plot Your Progress

IGHT THERAPY, MEDICATION, COUNSEL-
ling, exercise and diet are all well-acknowledged
ways of treating SAD and the seasonal blues.
The treatment or combination of treatments that works
best is different for everyone, so you might need to experiment for a while before you perfect your own
routine.

How can you accurately assess whether you are win-
ning the fight against SAD? If your doctor has you on
medication or if you are in a supervised light therapy
program, you will likely be assessed from time to time
by a trained clinician using the modified Hamilton Depression Rating Scale mentioned in Chapter 2 or some
similar assessment tool. Your score will tell the tale.

But what if you are self-treating milder SAD, the seasonal blues, with exercise and/or diet? How can you
come up with a reasonably objective assessment of your
progress? A weekly weigh-in on the bathroom scales
will measure the effectiveness of your diet and exercise regime. Is there a comparable mental weigh-in you
can perform to test whether or not you are making
progress against depression?

Depression can generate a mental fog that clouds
your mind and makes it difficult to concentrate and
think productively. Your level of alertness is dulled.
What you need is a test that will show to what degree

your level of alertness fluctuates in a single day. This test should be repeated every day or two so that an overall trend toward a lifting or densening of your mental fog is revealed.

Here is what you need to do. When you awaken in the morning, sit down with a book, a sheet of paper, a pen or pencil and a timing device that can be set to ring after an interval of 30 seconds. (A microwave oven is great for this, but don't forget to put something like a cup of water inside first.) Set the timer in motion, then open the book to a random page, write down the page number on your sheet of paper and close the book. Continue opening the book, jotting down random page numbers, then closing the book until the timer sounds.

Now count up the number of page numbers you were able to write down in the 30-second interval. On the first of the accompanying charts, find your score along the left-hand side of the chart, then move to the right until you reach the time of morning you per- formed this exercise and place a small X in this spot. You will want to repeat the entire process at one-hour intervals throughout your waking day. During the night, or at any time during the day when you are asleep, mark Xs down at the zero score level. It is rea- sonably safe to assume you are not alert at these times!

What you have now is a graphic display of the time(s) of day you are most alert and a record of your sleep pattern. The most common pattern is to score rela- tively low first thing in the morning, peak around 10 a.m., slump in mid to late afternoon, then peak again late in the evening.

# DON'T BE SAD

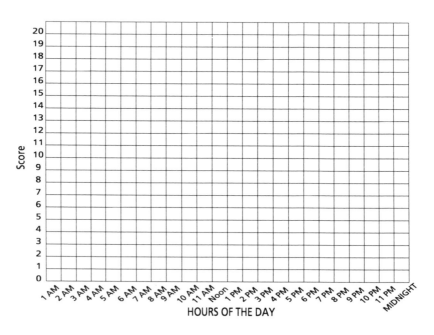

HOURS OF THE DAY

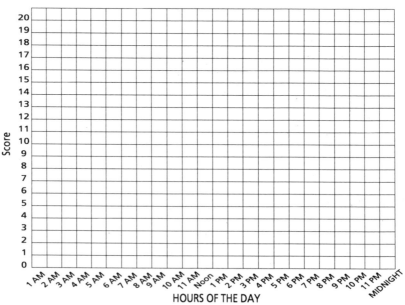

HOURS OF THE DAY

You can get revealing answers to two important questions by analyzing your personal chart.

1. How should you organize your day to best advantage?

   Look at the time (or times) of day when you are most alert. This is when you should try to accomplish your most demanding tasks. Set aside any repetitive busy work for the part of the day when you are in an alertness slump.

2. Is your current treatment regime doing you any good?

   Carry out this 24-hour test every four or five days over the next two to three weeks, assuming you are just beginning treatment. (A time span of less than two weeks will not give a new treatment regime a

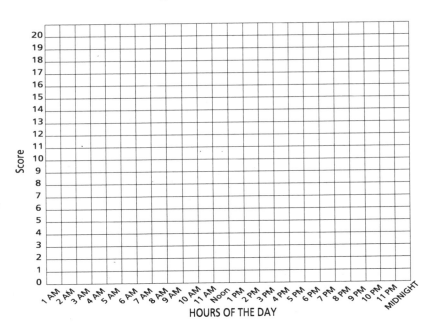

fair chance to show results.) Now compare your peak and slump scores on each successive test. If there is an overall trend toward higher scores as the weeks pass, your mental fog is lifting. Your treatment is working!

If your scores remain the same or show an overall tendency to drop, your treatment regime isn't coming through. Try changing one or more elements; for example, increase the amount of time you spend outdoors or in front of your light box every day. Now repeat the test over the next few weeks and note if there is any improvement in your score.

If your scores are not improving and your chart reveals that you are still sleeping an excessive amount, there is another avenue of attack open to you. Don't give in to your urge to sleep. Studies have shown it is possible to pull yourself out of a depressive mood and increase your energy levels by restricting to the norm the number of hours you sleep. This means falling asleep no later than 10 p.m. and getting up no later than 7 a.m. Try this and you should see improvement within a week!

# CHAPTER 13

# Adapt Your Environment

**Y**OU MIGHT NOT HAVE CONTROL OVER the climate or the amount of available sunshine outdoors, but you are boss inside your home, apartment or office. There are numerous changes, both subtle and dramatic, you can implement that will help alleviate the winter blues.

## Natural Lighting

Let's begin with the location and size of windows. You want lots of them, big, preferably facing south. It is obvious that the larger your window, the more light you will have falling into your room, but why is a southern exposure optimal? Where we live, here in the mid to high latitudes of the northern hemisphere, the sun rises in the east then arcs across the southern half of the sky and sets in the west. The highest point the sun reaches along its daily path varies with the seasons. In the summer, the sun peaks high overhead. In the winter, it hangs low in the south at noonday, and never rises at all north of the Arctic Circle. In other words, the sun is in the southeast, south, and southwest most of the time. So if you are out to capture as much sunshine as possible, you want south-facing windows.

One word of warning. Along with sunshine comes heat. You will want some sort of window treatment — blinds, heavy curtains, an outdoor awning — that can be employed during the heat of summer to lessen the amount of intense sunshine coming in, but can also be cleared out of the way during the winter months when you want all the light you can get. There are two other ways of dealing with this problem.

One is to plant a deciduous tree in the yard south of your window. In the summer its leaves act as a shade and in winter its bare branches let through all the wonderful sunlight. The other way of dealing with the varying sun angle can come into play if you are remodeling

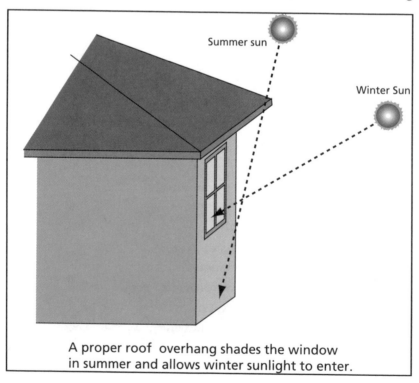

A proper roof overhang shades the window
in summer and allows winter sunlight to enter.

your home or building anew. Simply have your architect work out the width of roof overhang required at your latitude to keep the direct rays of the summer sun from falling into your room.

What about those windows that don't have southern exposures? East and west facing windows will capture direct sunlight half the day. But in the midst of winter, when the days are less than ten hours long, and grey at that, these windows are hardly optimal. And northern windows? Well, unless they look out onto a scene that reflects a great deal of light, such as a light-colored neighboring building or a field of snow, they are pretty useless from a SAD perspective.

# Artificial Lighting

So much for the limitations of natural lighting. The logical way to cope, assuming window orientation is not in your favor, is to incorporate artificial bright lights in your indoor environment. Here, the decorating possibilities are limitless. There are only two rules of thumb you must keep in mind: the light fixture(s) should provide an illumination level no lower than 2,500 lux and be situated close enough to the area in which you plan to spend the most time to deliver this level of light. The light fixture and your relaxation space or work space should be no more than three feet apart and the light box should be situated in such a way that you can easily glance at it once every 30 seconds or so. Don't hang a 2,500-lux light box at ceiling height and then arrange the furniture so that you sit nine feet away in a chair only two feet off the floor.

## Case Study: MARGE Takes Charge

Around the house, Marge (see Chapter 6) opens all the windows and has every light on all day long. At work, she's installed full-spectrum light bulbs in the fixtures.

"**Look for the light every day**," advises Marge, referring to more than just optical light. "Look for a smile or something else positive and hold onto that. Remember what it feels like to be happy."

If you are trying to introduce more light into your place of work, you will of course wish to take the comfort of your fellow workers into account and limit the area illuminated to simply your "space," assuming your workmates are not SAD people too! Both free-standing floor and table-top models of light boxes are available, as are special lamps, so it should not be difficult to fit one of these into your decor.

Cool-white fluorescent bulbs are often used in light box fixtures. However, if you enjoy the presence of greenery in your indoor environment, you might want to consider the use of full-spectrum light bulbs. These come much closer to mimicking the range of colors inherent in natural sunlight and plants tend to grow well in their vicinity. Full-spectrum light does contain a small amount of ultraviolet, but no more so than natural sunshine. However, if you burn easily in the sun, you might want to wear a light sunscreen if you spend long hours under these lights. Some SAD patients have reported slight tanning as a side effect of light therapy with full-spectrum lights.

*Note of caution: Full-spectrum lights are not the same as the lights used in tanning salons, which contain considerable amounts of UV and would be quite dangerous to both eyes and skin if used for purposes of light therapy.*

# The SAD Sanctuary

In addition to the use of natural and artificial lighting in your home or office, there are several other decorating measures you can try to banish gloom from inside your "built" environment. You might want to put these throughout your house, or designate one room that is

your place to go for a mood boost when you are feeling SAD or blue, your very own sanctuary.

The ambiance you are trying to create in this room is the light, warmth and cheery optimism of a bright spring day. At best your room has a large, south-facing window or a combination of lighting fixtures and windows facing other exposures.

If you are good with a paintbrush, likely the least expensive decor pick-me-up is the application of a cheery, light-colored coat of paint to the walls. White, pale beige or pastel shades of your favorite hue reflect a greater percentage of light back into the room and your eyes than dark colors. They also make the walls

## Case Study: JERRIE's Place

Jerrie, a lab technician in her early fifties, recently purchased a home. Having been on Prozac for SAD over the past few years, she knew that medication and light therapy were standard treatments for the syndrome but she had not been instructed in lifestyle changes that could make a difference. Even so, she instinctively painted all the walls and trim in in her new home light colors. She also set one room aside as "Jerrie's Place," a brightly lit and gayly decorated den where she can sit undisturbed and relax. Many SAD people, such as Jerrie, independently develop a keen sense of what works for them.

of a room appear to recede, creating the illusion of a larger space. Dark colors, on the other hand, bring the walls in closer, destroying the illusion you are attempting to imitate.

The use of bold color accents in furniture, upholstery and pillows can approximate the fresh, lively colors of spring flowers. You might also wish to cover your sofa or a chair in a cheery floral pattern, hang paintings or photographs of outdoor scenes on the walls, or even "force" daffodils and other spring bulbs to grow and flower during the winter months.

## Case Study: GLADYS

*"The Dance of Spring is the Dance of Life* is the title of the beautiful spring scene on a poster hanging over our fireplace," writes Gladys from Stratford, Ontario. "It must be May because the trees are bursting with young green foliage, there are brilliant white and fuchsia blossoms, and central to the whole picture is the bubbling happiness of a swollen spring stream."

# CHAPTER 14

# Follow the Sun

**M**ANY OF US INSTINCTIVELY FLEE the frozen North when cabin fever strikes in mid-winter. Favorite destinations of Canadian "snowbirds" who fly south for the winter are Florida, the deserts of the U.S. Southwest and sunny California. SAD members of the Mood Disorders Association of British Columbia polar bear swim group take a winter dip at Waikiki Beach every year rather than follow the lead of their neighbors, who prefer to remain home and dip their toes in the frigid waters off the coast of Vancouver on New Year's Day.

Travel is a great way to banish the winter blues (if you have the time and money). Within a few days of arriving at a destination situated in a sunny locale, many SAD people begin to shed their symptoms. They remain well as long as the vacation lasts and, if their SAD is the manic-depressive variety, they might even find themselves experiencing the symptoms of spring mania. Unfortunately, the benefits of a sunny holiday are transient. Within a few days of returning home, the same old SAD symptoms set in again.

If you find a spot in the world you are particularly taken with, a place where you feel so wonderful you begin to consider moving there, think this over carefully. Yes, the friendly climate could help alleviate your symptoms of SAD, but the stress of the move, the possible isolation from friends and family, the change of job or career this might entail could result in enough stress, anxiety and homesickness to cancel the light-given benefits. If you're tempted anyway, take things slowly. Make more than one trip to the place at different times of the year to be certain it is indeed someplace you would enjoy living year round. And beware. You could be seeing things through rose-colored glasses in the light of a manic swing.

## Case Study: DOLORES's Desert Dessert

A few years ago, Dolores and her husband took a trip south to explore the barren but exquisite scenery of Lake Mead in southern Nevada. It was the first week in April. The sky was clear and there was the abundance of hot, bright sunshine normally associated with desert climes.

Registering somewhere between the seasonal blues and full-blown SAD, Dolores had shunned her husband's amorous advances all winter. But one afternoon, a few days following their arrival, she found herself in a rather desperate state of mind. She reports that, while out on a drive, she began secretly scouting about for a nice secluded spot where they could pull over and make whoopee among the cacti. Her totally unsuspecting husband was saved only by the fact the entire countryside was crawling with other tourists and such a place could not be found.

# CHAPTER 15

# Helping Your SAD Spouse or Friend

**T**HIS CHAPTER IS FOR THE FRIENDS AND relatives of those who get either the seasonal blues or full-blown SAD. Relationships are often the first line of casualties in the battle against sea-

---

## Case Study: SIMON

"SAD puts a lot of strain on the relationship, especially at first, when your spouse's personality changes and they turn into a lump that won't get up off the couch," claims Simon, whose wife has suffered from SAD for many years.

"The first year, I was in shock. The second and third years, **I kept thinking 'I don't know how I can deal with this.'** Now I don't take it personally any more," says Simon. "When her mood drops, I just say 'Time to get your medication adjusted, dear.'"

At first, their three children were taking it personally, like Simon. He explained it wasn't their fault Mommy was sick. They shouldn't feel bad when their attempts to make her happy failed.

His wife admits Simon can see changes in her behavior she is totally unaware of. "My wife doesn't always realize what's going on," says Simon. "Sometimes she thinks the winter hasn't been too bad. I know otherwise."

---

sonal affective disorder. It's not easy living or working with someone who is depressed and withdrawn. In numerous SAD cases marriages break up, long-standing friendships fall apart and jobs are lost. It is truly tragic, because none of these things have to happen.

To this point, you have seen how light therapy, medications, counselling and lifestyle changes can be used successfully in the treatment of SAD. But one more component is critical — the support and understanding of friends and family.

The first and most crucial step in the management of this emotional roller coaster ride is recognizing and accepting the fact someone you care about has seasonal affective disorder. This person is not sulking around the house, falling asleep on the job, or shunning your sexual advances deliberately. This person is ill and needs your help.

If you are the spouse of a SAD person, you have experienced the consequences of your partner's annual changes in mood, energy level and behavior more than anyone else. Aside from keeping in mind the fact that

### Case Study: PAULA's Viewpoint

Paula (see Chapter 9), now successfully on Prozac, says she's grateful for all the years her family put up with her bad mood. "I blamed them for my SADness, so I wasn't very nice to them," she says with regret. "After I got on Prozac, I perceived a tremendous improvement in the way they were treating me, but I now realize it was actually a change in the way I was treating them!"

your spouse's symptoms are temporary and will pass with the seasons, what can you do to minimize the negative impact of SAD on your relationship?

• **Gear up in advance.**

This is one syndrome you can actually predict, so make the most of this. There are a few things you can do early in the fall to help the two of you get over the initial hurdle when depression sets in.

If you are planning to administer light treatments at home, ensure your light therapy equipment is in proper working order. Agree in advance on a spot in the house where the light box can remain set up throughout the winter without interfering with anyone's lifestyle.

Discuss now how you will handle the holidays so you both take the same tack when relatives and friends call to make plans. Do you really have to play host to the entire family? How much shopping, cooking and

---

**Case Study: SIMON's Dilemma**

Simon's wife sought relief from her SADness through the use of both medication and light therapy. Simon wanted her to benefit from the therapeutic value of her light box, but it caused him a good deal of grief when she first brought it home.

"When she first began using the light box at home, it drove me crazy," says Simon. "I work nights. Having light that bright indoors during the day was very disturbing." Simon has since found it helps to avert his vision from the light when he talks to his wife during her treatments.

entertaining will you realistically be capable of taking on between the two of you if one won't be operating on all eight cylinders? Perhaps there is still time to book a nice sunny vacation.

• **Minimize stress.**

Both you and your SAD spouse will experience less frustration if you do your best to minimize stressful situations. You can help by easing up on your expectations of what your spouse is capable of accomplishing during a depressive episode.

— Don't expect your spouse to be at your side and cheery on every social occasion that crops up. You might have to decline an invitation once in a while or go solo.

— Don't expect your spouse to maintain his or her usual standard of commitment to household chores, child rearing and career. In the larger picture, does it really matter if the furniture is dusty, if the kids can't have their friends over to play every day after school, or if your spouse uses up "vacation days" to stay home from work when he or she runs out of "sick days"?

— Don't expect your spouse to be attentive to your sexual needs. This is a difficult one, but try. Your spouse really has lost his or her interest in sex and is feeling far too tired, to boot. The hardest part is managing not to show your disappointment. If your partner senses they have let you down, this could trigger a vicious bout of self-recrimination and guilt, leading to deeper depression.

And the biggest don't of all . . .

• **Don't be critical.**

Yes, you are seeing someone you love transform before your eyes into a different person. Their weight is changing. They have no enthusiasm for participating in the activities you have always done as a couple. They're irritable and grumpy for no apparent reason.

But you know what is happening. And that puts an onus on you to be as supportive and uncritical as possible. People who are depressed do not always respond to criticism, even constructive criticism, in a rational manner. If you berate them for overeating, they are more likely to dwell on feelings of worthlessness while downing another donut than contemplate going on a diet.

• **Be on the alert.**

The feelings of guilt, self-recrimination, worthlessness and hopelessness associated with depression can sometimes swell to dangerous proportions. Never ignore the mention or threat of suicide. If someone has reached the point where they are capable of expressing such thoughts, they may be on the road to executing them. **Seek psychiatric help immediately.**

This is one area where health care professionals are a *necessity*, as much for your sake as for the safety of the potentially suicidal person. If you and your family try to deal with the situation unaided and fail, it can leave life-long mental scars on those involved.

• **Be on the watch for spring mania.**

Often the manic behavior of the Spring Swing causes as many social and relationship problems as the depression of winter. If your spouse or friend becomes cheery and slightly euphoric with the arrival of spring, this is to be expected and welcomed. But if he or she becomes manic, their inappropriate behavior can present a real threat to your relationship, pocketbook and mutual well-being.

In the midst of their mania, everything is likely to look just dandy. There is no need for help that the SAD person can see. So it is up to others to monitor the situation and ensure things don't get out of hand. **Seeing that your partner receives immediate professional help at this time is as important as obtaining assistance for the depression of winter.**

Here are a few tell-tale signs of mania you should watch for.

— Non-stop talking: Is this the same withdrawn, listless person you've failed all winter to pry more than three words out of at a time? Just try getting two words in edgewise now! The chatter is continuous and not always rational. Your partner may be in the midst of an animated, breathless description of some great project they have taken on when, suddenly, they go off talking to themselves on a seemingly unconnected topic.

— Excessive activity: Can you (or any mortal being) keep up with the pace your spouse has set? Projects at home and at work, social engagements and recreational activities are tackled in rapid succession or often simultaneously. When it comes right down to the bottom line, however, productivity doesn't necessarily measure up to the amount of effort put into the day's activities. No one project is the focus of attention long enough to get results. Your partner is like a busy bee flitting from flower to flower, dawn until dusk (and then some), industriously gathering pollen but never bothering to return to the hive to deposit the fruits of its labor. This behavior can be exhausting, so don't be surprised if your spouse begins to show symptoms of fatigue like those experienced during the winter.

— Overspending: Budget? What's a budget? Your partner *wants* that antique rocking chair, top-of-the-line golf club set, or Afghan hound. Someone else can worry about how to pay for it when the bill arrives — that someone more likely than not being you. The trick here is in catching this type of behavior before your partner expends your household income for the next year all in one fell swoop.

— Promiscuity: Good judgement is not a strong trait of someone in the manic state. All manner of inappropriate behavior can crop up. Perhaps your partner insists on being the center of attention in social situations, to the point of making a fool of themselves.

Worse yet, your manic spouse might lose all sight of marital vows and sexual discretion. The same person who had no interest in sex at all just weeks before can suddenly be on the prowl. This is potentially dangerous for both of you in this day of AIDS and other sexually-transmitted diseases.

Speed in obtaining professional medical help as soon as manic behavior is detected, along with an understanding that it is part and parcel of your partner's mood disorder, can go a long way toward preventing irreparable damage to your relationship.

# PART 4

# Why You're SAD

Seasonal affective disorder is a real medical condition. It is well defined and easily diagnosed. There are identifiable environmental triggers and proven courses of treatment. Yet we are still in the dark when it comes to the question of exactly what causes SAD.

We need to be specific when we ask this question. Are we referring to winter SAD or summer SAD? The two disorders appear to have completely different underlying causes. Research has barely scratched the surface of summer SAD, so the following discussion will focus exclusively on what we know about the cause of winter SAD. Numerous observations and clinical studies support the concept that light is the core problem.

# CHAPTER 16

# Light: A Feast for the Eyes

**L**IGHT, SHADOW, COLOR, FORM. OUR EYES are remarkable sense organs that collect incredible amounts of information every second — important data received as discrete packets of light energy called "photons."

The amount of energy any one photon carries with it depends on the wavelength, or color, of light it constitutes. Under normal conditions, the visual part of the electromagnetic spectrum starts in the high-energy, short wavelength violet light around 4000 Ångstroms and ends in the lower-energy, longer wavelength red light around 7000 Ångstroms. (One Ångstrom is equal to one hundred-millionth of a meter.) All the colors of the rainbow extend between these two extremes.

When light enters the eye, it falls on the retina at the back of the eyeball. The surface of the retina is covered

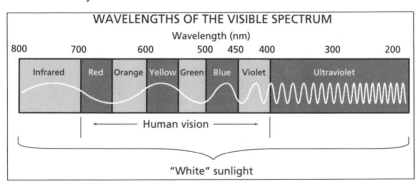

WAVELENGTHS OF THE VISIBLE SPECTRUM

with rods and cones, the eye's light detectors, which convert each photon of light into an electrochemical impulse that travels along the optic nerve deep into the brain where it stimulates the hypothalamus and pineal gland.

The hypothalamus is especially important in the study of seasonal affective disorder because it is involved directly or indirectly in the regulation of most of the body's endocrine functions — and it takes its regulatory cues from light. When the electrochemical signals initiated in the retina by the reception of light arrive at the hypothalamus, they trigger synthesis of several neurotransmitters (chemical messengers). The two most closely associated with affective disorders are the neurotransmitters norepinephrine and serotonin. They affect mood, appetite, sleep patterns, energy levels and libido — our very line-up of SAD symptoms.

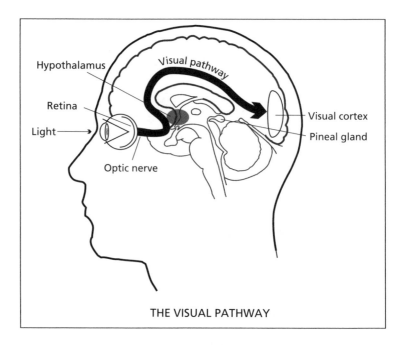

THE VISUAL PATHWAY

# CHAPTER 17

# Tripping (Over) the Lights Fantastic

CATCHING THE BIOLOGICAL CULPRIT RE-sponsible for seasonal affective disorder is not an easy task. False starts and temporary dead ends litter the pursuit up until now.

At present, there are four basic theories on the table for consideration. One has to do with internal biological clocks that might be out of sync with one another in SAD individuals. Two theories tackle the way light is processed on the retina of the eye, its point of entry. And the last looks at how the biochemicals that affect mood and appetite are generated in SAD and non-SAD brains.

As you will see, each theory has its strengths and weaknesses. It is highly unlikely any one of these four approaches constitutes the sole solution to the SAD puzzle. More likely than not, the ultimate answer, when it is found, will incorporate aspects of all four.

## The Timing is All Wrong

When researchers first began looking for the underlying cause of seasonal affective disorder, they turned their attention to chronobiology, the study of our internal biological clocks.

Have you ever wondered why you normally fall asleep at night, not during the day? What about jet lag?

Why does your body insist on keeping pace with the time zone in which your travel originated . . . and why does it come around to local time after a day or two has passed? Or, on a different note entirely, have you ever noticed how your fingernails grow at a regular pace? Biological functions like these all require constant regulation. They rely on internal timing mechanisms in the brain we are totally unconscious of most of the time.

Our internal clocks keep our bodily functions in harmony with three different time cycles: the 24-hour day (circadian rhythm), the month and the year (circannual rhythm). A specialized portion of the hypothalamus gland in the brain synchronizes our internal clocks with one another, with the external cycles of night and day and with the seasons by picking up clues from the environment. Primary among these clues are changes in temperature and light.

The chronobiology theory of seasonal affective disorder has gone through a few revisions over the years. In its original form, it assumed SAD people become depressed during the winter due to a disturbance in their circadian rhythms — their internal sleep clock gets out of sync with the daily pattern of light and dark.

Researchers can detect the improper setting of the internal clock that regulates sleep in SAD patients by measuring levels of the hormone melatonin. The amount of melatonin present in your body varies during the day. During daytime hours, the level of melatonin is normally quite low. Once the sun has set in the evening, the pineal gland in your brain begins to produce greater amounts of melatonin and your biological clock responds by preparing you for the onset of sleep. Bright daylight acts as the main environmental cue that keeps the circadian cycle in sync with day and night, and melatonin provides internal feedback to keep the system stable.

Early in the study of seasonal affective disorder, researchers speculated melatonin must play a major role in SAD. They watched for the point late in the day when SAD patients began to produce more melatonin and found it lagged behind normal circadian rhythms. Furthermore, light therapy studies showed bright light treatment in the morning hours could put the patients' biological clock back on track, whereas bright light in the evening made things worse. Was an improperly set biological clock throwing SAD people into a state of depression by altering normal sleep patterns? The results of initial studies looked promising, but further research does not appear to uphold this theory.

In one instance, a study similar to the melatonin level observations was carried out on

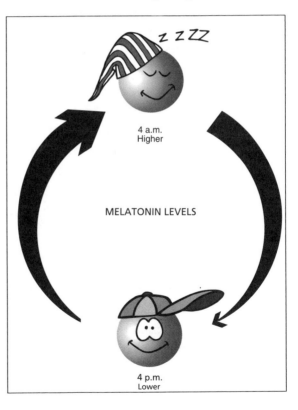

4 a.m.
Higher

MELATONIN LEVELS

4 p.m.
Lower

a group of non-SAD individuals stationed in the Antarctic during the dark months of Antarctic winter. They exhibited a lag in their biological clock similar to the lag seen in SAD patients. These non-SAD individuals slept long hours and woke up late in the morning, yet they did not show symptoms of depression. In another study, SAD patients treated with light therapy came out of their depression but did not experience a resetting of their haywire biological clock.

And what about the light therapy studies that indicated morning treatment was preferable to evening treatment, as would be predicted by the chronobiology theory? Subsequent studies and analysis of the way the original research was carried out have invalidated the earlier results. The recipients of light therapy in the initial studies were given the morning treatment for a set number of weeks, then were put on the evening treatment for a second go around. We now know that in "crossover" tests of this sort it is not unusual for participants to rate the effectiveness of the first treatment higher than that of the second round of treatment. Studies designed to avoid this pitfall show light therapy works equally well at **any** time of the day. There appears to be no cause-and-effect relationship between SAD and out-of-sync internal clocks.

In light of these contradictions, Dr. Alfred J. Lewy at the University of Oregon (the leading proponent of the chronobiology theory) has proposed an alteration to the original hypothesis. He now speculates SAD is brought about when your internal sleep clock becomes out of sync with the internal clocks regulating other bodily functions. How well your *internal* sleep clock keeps step with the *external* daily cycle is no longer considered to be a factor.

There is support for the concept that melatonin is implicated to some degree in the underlying cause of SAD. A recent test of the drug propranolol, which prevents synthesis of melatonin, showed some promise when administered to SAD patients in the morning.

# Fill'er Up!

A little low on light today? Just turn on the bulbs and top up your levels.

This second SAD theory proposes that a certain quantifiable amount of light is required on a regular basis to stave off depression in people who have seasonal affective disorder. It is not particularly important how bright the light you are exposed to is, or what time of day you take light treatments. What is critical is that, over the course of the day, the retinas in your eyes are bombarded by a set minimum number of photons.

The total amount of light you are exposed to in winter simply does not meet this requirement. There are precious few hours of bright daylight and the low-wattage artificial bulbs most people function under during the dark hours are feeble. So your SAD symptoms set in on a regular basis as the days grow shorter.

Clinical trials would seem to substantiate the idea that your daily dose of light can be "topped up" to useful levels through light therapy. Remember how light therapy treatments using 2,500-lux units usually require two hours to be effective, whereas treatments employing 10,000-lux units need only 30 minutes? These results fall right in line with what this theory would predict: the brighter the light, the more quickly the critical dose of photons is attained.

As promising as the photon theory looked for many years, it's recently run into one little snag.

How can it account for the success of dim light treatment obtained using light visors or dawn simulation therapy? How can 30 minutes exposure to the dim red light-emitting diodes used in some visors possibly deliver the same quantity of photons to your eyes as 30 minutes exposure to a 10,000-lux light box?

These are difficult questions to which proponents of the photon theory are currently scrambling to find answers.

## Sometimes You're Just Too Insensitive

It has been known for quite some time that individuals with manic-depressive disorders are supersensitive to light. People with seasonal affective disorder exhibit many of the same symptoms as manic-depressives. Might SAD people have a problem with sensitivity to light as well?

The conundrum here lies in determining whether SAD eyes are supersensitive, like manic-depressive eyes, or subsensitive—which would appear to be the more logical explanation of the two. If SAD people were subsensitive to light, their eyes would be inefficient light processors. They would require exposure to larger quantities of light than non-SAD people, just to come through the day having processed the same number of photons. This is similar to a person with respiratory problems who requires extra oxygen in order to keep going. SAD people's inability to process normal amounts of light would become particularly critical during the short, dark days of winter.

The subsensitivity theory has received supporting evidence from several studies. Dr. Raymond Lam and his colleagues in Vancouver have measured the light sensitivity of retinas in both SAD and non-SAD individuals. Their data show that SAD eyes are indeed subsensitive to light. When a photon is processed in the eye's retina, the cone or rod that detected the light requires "resetting" so that it can process subsequent photons that come its way. In SAD individuals, this automatic resetting mechanism fails.

Dr. Lam speculates exposure to adequate amounts of bright light might force this resetting mechanism back into action. Once the sensitivity of SAD eyes is restored, the symptoms of seasonal affective disorder disappear. He also points out that subsensitivity to light might account for the lag in circadian rhythms observed in SAD people. If SAD eyes are not processing light efficiently, the signal to the brain that synchronizes the internal biological clock might be too weak to work. Perhaps light therapy is effective because it provides enough bright light to send an adequately strong signal and pull all the rhythms into sync with one another.

But what about the manic-depressives? How can their depression be caused by a supersensitivity to light while the depression of SAD is caused by a subsensitivity to light? According to Dr. Lam, tests have shown that people with nonseasonal depression do not respond as quickly or as dramatically to bright light exposure as people with seasonal affective disorder. This leads him to believe an entirely different retinal mechanism is malfunctioning in the case of manic-depressives.

Objections to the subsensitivity theory of SAD include evidence collected by Dr. Chris Thompson in Great Britain that SAD individuals are supersensitive to light in the winter and subsensitive in the summer — just the reverse of what one would expect. And, once again, how can subsensitivity to light explain why dim light therapy works?

# It's All in the Chemistry

Our bodies are like giant chemistry sets. Unconsciously, every day, we are busy putting together and breaking apart a wide array of biochemicals, such as hormones and neurotransmitters. In order to maintain our physical and mental health, exactly the right amount of each biochemical must be produced and, once produced, each must be utilized properly within our systems.

It is becoming increasingly clear that something is wrong with levels of the neurotransmitter serotonin in SAD and blue people. Serotonin plays an important role in the normal functioning of our bodies. Among other things, it is involved in the regulation of sleep, appetite and weight. Too much serotonin can initiate the onset of sleep, perhaps leading to the hypersomnia experienced by SAD people. Too little serotonin can bring about the carbohydrate craving and weight gain seen in SAD.

Serotonin levels vary in a regular pattern over the course of the year. Levels consistently drop through fall and winter and reach their lowest point in early spring.

Because this corresponds with the time of year when the greatest frequency of suicides occur, researchers have speculated seasonal serotonin fluctuations might be related to seasonal changes in mood.

Serotonin is generated in both the central nervous system and the hypothalamus gland of the brain. Direct measurement of serotonin levels is difficult, so an indirect approach is normally used. Amounts of cortisol and/or prolactin in the blood (two hormones secreted in proportion to the level of serotonin in the body) are measured instead.

Research carried out by Dr. Norman Rosenthal and his colleagues has revealed some interesting differences between the way serotonin functions in SAD and non-SAD people. When administered serotonin in the form of m-CPP (m-chlorophenylpiperazine, the active metabolite in the antidepressant drug trazodone), SAD and non-SAD people report a different subjective response. People with SAD find it makes them feel absolutely euphoric, whereas non-SAD people experience a sense of being "slowed down." Significantly, after receiving light treatment, SAD people's depressive symptoms lift and they report feeling "slowed down" by m-CPP, just like non-SAD people.

This is similar to the reactions observed in another study headed by Dr. Rosenthal. SAD and non-SAD people were asked to evaluate how they felt after eating a carbohydrate-loaded meal. Many SAD people reported feeling energized whereas non-SAD people became drowsy.

Dr. Rosenthal suggests SAD people might be super-sensitive to changes in serotonin levels in their brains.

Serotonin is one of the neurotransmitters produced in response to light. In the winter, there is insufficient bright light available to trigger synthesis of sufficient levels of serotonin in SAD individuals. As the days get shorter, their serotonin level drops and so does their mood. They respond abnormally to the increased serotonin level brought about through carbohydrate consumption because the sites in the body that receive and process serotonin have been sensitized by pro-longed underexposure to this neurotransmitter and they overreact when it finally shows up. Light therapy cor-rects this supersensitivity by getting serotonin levels back up where they should be.

The concept that serotonin has a role in the underly-ing cause of SAD has gained additional support from a recent positron emission tomography (PET) study car-ried out at the National Institute of Mental Health. This remarkable research technique provides images of thin cross-sectional slices of the working human brain, show-ing the areas that are active at the time of the PET scan.

Dr. Robert M. Cohen and his colleagues at NIMH did PET scans on groups of SAD and non-SAD individuals in order to compare how their brains might differ in the way they work. Among other things, the researchers determined that the neurotransmitter serotonin regu-lates some regions of the brain which their tests indicated function differently in SAD individuals. Overall, they concluded SAD brains appear to be less capable of ac-knowledging environmental cues, such as light, and are less able to sustain goal-oriented behavior.

# CHAPTER 18

# Conclusion

**B**ARELY MORE THAN ONE DECADE HAS gone by since Dr. Norman Rosenthal and his colleagues at the National Institute of Mental Health in Bethesda, Maryland, first defined seasonal affective disorder and made the syndrome a focus of modern medical attention and research. Not long at all in the grand scheme of things.

One of the most intriguing aspects of SAD is the fact it reflects the degree to which we, as humans, are affected by our external environment. Until recently, medical research traditionally looked to the interior environment, the world of the human body, for causes of disease. The concept that humans respond to and, in fact, rely on external environmental cues to maintain health is only now gaining widespread acceptance.

And just in time.

Acknowledgement of our dependency on environmental factors is critical to our well-being now and in the future. At present, large numbers of people live and work in artificial environments that isolate them from nature with little or no regard to the effects this lifestyle might have on the individual. As we learn more about the intricate ways in which our bodies have evolved to cope with and take advantage of the external environment, the attitude that we can simply turn our backs on nature is changing, but slowly.

The extent to which we are truly products of our earthly environment will become even more pronounced in the future. As humans move into space, it will become critical to understand all the ways in which we have adapted to the rhythms and resources of our home planet. How will we ensure the internal clocks of space station crew members are supplied with essential timing cues unless we understand what those cues are? The research into seasonal affective disorder is only one of many steps being taken in this direction.

Given the relatively short time period this research has been going on, it is not surprising there are still many questions regarding the biological mechanism of SAD left unanswered. But these gaps in our knowledge have not hampered the ability of scientists to find and develop a number of effective approaches to the treatment of seasonal affective disorder. Light therapy, medication, and diet all can play an important part in the management of this syndrome. There is plenty you can do. Don't be SAD any longer!

# GLOSSARY

**Ambient light** The light in your immediate surroundings.

**Attention deficit disorder** A syndrome characterized by a lack of ability to focus attention on a single task for any length of time. It is often, but not always, associated with hyperactivity. Other symptoms include impairment of memory, motor skills, speech, perception and conceptualization plus increased impulsiveness and emotionality. The disorder can affect people of any age but shows up most often among children, especially young males.

**Behavior therapy** A treatment for psychological disorders that focuses solely on identifying and altering inappropriate behavioral patterns. This form of therapy does not take into account the patient's emotions, ideas, mental state or unconscious mental processes. Rather, it achieves its end by encouraging automatic response to stimuli.

**Bipolar disorder** A major mood disorder in which the patient swings back and forth between the elevated mood of mania and the low mood of depression. "Bipolar I" disorder is distinguished by episodes of full-blown mania. "Bipolar II" disorder involves episodes of elevated mood that fall short of mania.

**Bulimia nervosa** An eating disorder distinguished by episodes of uncontrollable craving for food and binge eating. These episodes often are followed by self-induced purging (throwing up and enemas) and bouts of depression.

**Chronic Fatigue Syndrome** A collection of seemingly related symptoms, the most pronounced of which is prolonged extreme fatigue. There is still considerable controversy surrounding the validity of this syndrome.

**Circadian rhythm** A series of events that repeats on a 24-hour basis is said to be "circadian" (from the Latin *circa* = "about" and *dia* = "day"). In the context of human biology, the two most obvious circadian rhythms are sleeping and eating patterns.

**Cognitive therapy** The treatment of emotional and mental disorders by various means with the goal of changing a patient's way of thinking.

**Dawn simulation** A light therapy technique that mimics the gradually increasing illumination of natural dawn. The therapeutic dose of light inside the patient's bedroom is delivered in the morning while the patient is still asleep.

**Delta sleep** The deepest, most restful form of sleep. A person in delta sleep is in a state of dreamlessness and is not easy to awaken.

**Depression** A mood disorder associated with low mood, sadness, despair, low self-esteem, hopelessness, apathy and withdrawal. These psychological symptoms are sometimes accompanied by physiological symptoms such as fatigue and changes in sleep, appetite and/or sex drive.

**Depressive mood disorder** An emotional disorder characterized by recurrent episodes of depression (*see* "Depression").

**Diffusion screen** A piece of partially opaque material placed over a light source to disperse the light and provide an evenly illuminated surface. The diffusion screen also helps block passage of the harmful ultraviolet component of light.

**Fluorescent light** Light produced by a tube that is coated on the inside with a phosphor. The phosphor glows, or "fluoresces," in the presence of ultraviolet radiation or in the presence of an electric field.

**Full-spectrum light** Light produced by a source that emits all the colors of the visual spectrum in amounts that mimic the spectral energy output of natural sunlight.

**Glucose** A form of sugar found in many foods. It is a "simple" sugar which is easily and quickly used as an energy source once inside the body.

**Hypersomnia** A tendency to sleep for abnormally long amounts of time and/or experience extreme drowsiness. Psychological factors, rather than physical factors, are usually the cause of hypersomnia.

**Hypoglycemia** A condition brought about by abnormally low levels of glucose in the blood. Symptoms include headache, weakness, hunger, visual problems, altered personality and anxiety. Hypoglycemia may lead to coma or death if left untreated.

**Hypothyroidism** A condition resulting from reduced activity of the thyroid gland. Symptoms include weight gain, fatigue, arthritis and constipation. Like hypoglycemia (*see* "Hypoglycemia"), hypothyroidism can lead to coma or death if left untreated.

**Incandescent light** Light produced by the glowing of a white-hot filament inside a glass bulb evacuated of air.

**Light box**  A light source widely used in light therapy that consists of several fluorescent or full-spectrum bulbs mounted in a box and covered by a diffusion screen.

**Light therapy**  The administration of prescribed doses of light through the optic (visual) tract. Used to alleviate symptoms of seasonal affective disorder and a growing list of other syndromes, such as premenstrual syndrome and bulimia.

**Light visor**  A head-mounted, portable light source used in light therapy.

**Lux unit**  A unit of illumination used in the context of SAD to rate the amount of light delivered to your eyes by light therapy equipment.

**Mania**  A mood disorder at the opposite end of the emotional scale from depression. In the manic state a person generally displays elated mood, extreme talkativeness, hyperactivity, short attention span, agitation and fidgeting. Their behavior can become violent and sometimes self-destructive. Mania is one component of bipolar disorder, depression being the other component.

**Melatonin**  A hormone secreted into the bloodstream by the pineal gland that is suspected of being involved in some way with the underlying biological mechanism of SAD. Melatonin levels increase during the course of the evening and peak during the early hours before dawn. Levels fall off once the sun comes up or once a person begins their daily morning light therapy.

**Metabolism** The biochemical process that converts the nutrient content of food into forms of energy the body can use immediately or at some point in the future.

**Neurons** Nerve cells.

**Neurotransmitter** A chemical messenger that transfers nerve impulses from one nerve cell to another across the synaptic gap (*see* "Synaptic gap").

**Photon** A quantum unit, or basic "package" of light energy. The amount of energy carried in a photon depends on the color of light it constitutes.

**Phototherapy** (*see* "Light therapy")

**Placebo** An inactive treatment prescribed in clinical trials as if it were the active treatment under investigation. This shows how much of the recorded effectiveness of the treatment under investigation is likely real and how much is imagined due to preconceived expectations of the trial participants.

**Positron emission tomography (PET)** A computerized research technique for examining metabolic activity within the body. The patient inhales or is injected with a biochemical laced with a radioactive substance that emits positrons, positively-charged particles. The radioactive substance is transported to the area of the body under scrutiny, where the positrons it emits interact with electrons (negatively-charged particles) in the tissues. These positron-electron collisions generate gamma rays that are detected and recorded by the computer, which builds up detailed pictures based on the data.

**Psychoanalysis** A branch of psychology that helps patients identify unconscious drives or emotional conflicts and bring them into the realm of the conscious mind where they can be analyzed and modified.

**SAD** Acronym for seasonal affective disorder

**Seasonal blues** A term used to describe the non-clinical, less debilitating form of seasonal affective disorder. Generally, someone with the seasonal blues may suffer from the symptoms of SAD to one degree or another but *does not* experience episodes of depression lasting two weeks or longer.

**Serotonin** The neurotransmitter most closely implicated in the underlying mechanism of SAD. Serotonin is active in the regulation of appetite, sleep and mood — three core symptoms of SAD.

**Start-up time** The time that elapses between beginning a medication and first benefitting from it.

**Synaptic gap (or cleft)** The extremely minute space between the sending end of one nerve cell and the receiving end of another. Nerve impulses are transported across this gap by special messenger chemicals called neurotransmitters.

**Syndrome** A group of symptoms brought about by a common underlying cause.

**Ultraviolet (UV)** The high-energy, short wavelengths of light just beyond the violet portion of the visual color spectrum.

**Vegan** A strict vegetarian who, in addition to avoiding animal flesh, does not eat eggs or dairy products.

**Winter blues** The winter form of seasonal blues (*see* "Seasonal blues").

# APPENDIX A

# Further Reading

The number of books and research articles published on the topic of seasonal affective disorder is enormous and growing all the time. The following list is partial and, for the most part, reflects works consulted in the preparation of *Don't Be SAD*.

## What Is SAD?

Allen J.M., Lam R.W., Remick R.A., Sadovnick A.D. "Depressive Symptoms and Family History in Seasonal and Nonseasonal Mood Disorders," *American Journal of Psychiatry*. Vol. 150:3, March 1993, p. 443.

American Psychiatric Association. *Diagnostic and Statistical Manual of Mental Disorders*, 4th edition, 1994. American Psychiatric Association Press, Washington, D.C.

Bauer M.S., Dunner D. "Validity of Seasonal Pattern as a Modifier for Recurrent Mood Disorders in DSM-IV," *Comprehensive Psychiatry*. May-June 1993, vol. 3, no. 3, pp. 159–170.

Carskadon M.A., Acebo C. "Parental Reports of Seasonal Mood and Behavior Changes in Children," *Journal of the American Academy of Child and Adolescent Psychiatry*. March 1993, vol. 32, no. 2, pp. 264-269.

Cohen R.M., Gross M., Nordahl T.E., Semple W.E., Oren D.A., Rosenthal N.E. "Preliminary Data on the Metabolic Brain Pattern of Patients with Winter Seasonal Affective Disorder," *Archives of General Psychiatry*. 1992, vol. 49, pp. 545–552.

Faedda G.L., Tondo L., Teicher M.H., Baldessarini R.J., Gelbard H.A. and Floris G.F. "Seasonal Mood Disorders: Patterns of Seasonal Recurrence in Mania and Depression," *Archive of General Psychiatry*. Vol. 50, January 1993, p. 17.

Gorman C.P., Wyse P.H., Demjen S., Caldwell L.H., Chorney M.Y., Samek N.P. "Ophthalmological Profile of 71 SAD Patients: A Significant Correlation Between Myopia and SAD" [Abstract], *Abstracts of the 5th Annual Meeting of the Society of Light Treatment and Biological Rhythms*. San Diego, June 1993:8.

Halle M.T., Dilsaver S.C. "Comorbid Panic Disorder in Patients with Winter Depression," *American Journal of Psychiatry*. Vol. 150:7, July 1993, p. 1108.

Hardin T.A., Wehr T.A., Brewerton T., Kasper S., Berrettini W., Rabkin J., Rosenthal N.E. "Evaluation of Seasonality in Six Clinical Populations and Two Normal Populations," *Journal of Psychiatric Research*. 1991, vol. 25, no. 3, pp. 75–87.

Joseph-Vanderpool J.R., Jacobsen F.M., Murphy D.L., Hill J.L., Rosenthal N.E. "Seasonal Variation in Behavioral Responses to m-CPP in Patients with Seasonal Affective Disorder and Controls," *Biological Psychiatry*. April 1, 1993, vol. 33, no. 7, pp. 496–504.

Lam R.W. "Seasonal Affective Disorder Presenting as Chronic Fatigue Syndrome," *Canadian Journal of Psychiatry*. 1991, vol. 36, pp. 680–682.

Lam R.W. "Seasonal Affective Disorder," *Current Opinion in Psychiatry*. 1994, vol. 7, pp. 9–13.

Lam R.W. "Seasonal Affective Disorder: Emerging from the Dark," *The Canadian Journal of Diagnosis*. January 1994, pp. 53–64.

Lam R.W., Beattie C.W., Buchanan A., Mador J.A. "Electroretinography in Seasonal Affective Disorder," *Psychiatry Research*. 1992, vol. 43, pp. 55–63.

Lam R.W., Buchanan A., Remick R.A. "Seasonal Affective Disorder — A Canadian Sample," *Annals of Clinical Psychiatry*. 1989, vol. 1, pp. 241–245.

Lam R.W. et. al. "Low Electrooculographic Ratios in Patients with Seasonal Affective Disorder," *American Journal of Psychiatry*. Vol. 148:11, November 1991, p. 1526.

Rosenthal N.E. "Diagnosis and Treatment of Seasonal Affective Disorder," *Journal of the American Medical Association* (JAMA). December 8, 1993, vol. 270, no. 22, p. 2717.

Rosenthal N.E. *Winter Blues: Seasonal Affective Disorder: What It Is and How to Overcome It.* Guilford Press, New York, 1993.

Rosenthal N.E., Bradt G.J., Wehr T.A. *Seasonal Pattern Assessment Questionnaire.* National Institute of Mental Health, Bethesda, Maryland, 1984.

Rosenthal N.E., Jacobsen F.M., Sack D.A., Arendt J., James S.P., Parry B.L., Wehr T.A. "Atenolol in Seasonal Affective Disorder: A Test of the Melatonin Hypothesis," *American Journal of Psychiatry.* January 1988, vol. 145, no. 1, pp. 52–56.

Rosenthal N.E., Sack D.A., Gillin J.C., Lewy A.J., Goodwin F.K., Davenport Y., Mueller P.S., Newsome D.A., Wehr T.A. "Seasonal Affective Disorder: A Description of the Syndrome and Preliminary Findings with Light Therapy," *Archives of General Psychiatry.* 1984, vol. 41, pp. 72–80.

Thompson C., Silverstone T. (editors). *Seasonal Affective Disorder.* CNS (Clinical Neuroscience) Publishers, London, 1989.

Wehr T.A., Giesen H.A., Schulz P.M., Anderson J.L., Joseph-Vanderpool J.R., Kelly K., Kasper S., Rosenthal N.E. "Contrasts Between Symptoms of Summer Depression and Winter Depression," *Journal of Affective Disorders.* December 1991, vol. 23, no. 4, pp. 173–183.

Wehr T.A., Sack D.A., Rosenthal N.E. "Seasonal Affective Disorder with Summer Depression and Winter Hypomania," *American Journal of Psychiatry.* Vol. 144, pp. 1602–1603.

Young M.A., Watel L.G., Lahmeyer H.W., Eastman C.I. "The Temporal Onset of Individual Symptoms in Winter Depression: Differentiating Underlying Mechanisms," *Journal of Affective Disorders.* August 1991, vol. 22, no. 4, pp. 191–197.

## Light Therapy

Avery D.H., Bolte M.A., Cohen S., Millet M.S. "Gradual Versus Rapid Dawn Simulation Treatment of Winter Depression," *Journal of Clinical Psychiatry.* 1992, vol. 53, pp. 359–363.

Avery D.H., Bolte M.A., Dager S.R., Wilson L.G., Weyer M., Cox G.B., Dunner D.L. "Dawn Simulation Treatment of Winter Depression: A Controlled Study," *American Journal of Psychiatry.* Vol. 150:1, January 1993, vol. 150, pp. 113–117.

Bielski R.J., Mayor J., Rice J. "Phototherapy with Broad Spectrum White Fluorescent Light: A Comparative Study," *Psychiatry Research*. Vol. 43, pp. 167–175.

Czeisler C.A., Allan J.S., Strogatz S.H., Ronda J.M., Sanchez R., Rios C.D., Freitag W.O., Richardson G.S., Kronauer R.E. "Bright Light Resets the Human Circadian Pacemaker Independent of the Timing of the Sleep-wake Cycle," *Science*. 1986, vol. 233, no. 4764, pp. 667-671.

Czeisler C.A., et. al. "Bright Light Induction of Strong (Type 0) Resetting of the Human Circadian Pacemaker," *Science*. Vol. 244, June 1989, p. 1328.

Eastman C.I., Gallo L.C., Lahmeyer H.W., Fogg L.F. "The Circadian Rhythm of Temperature During Light Treatment for Winter Depression," *Biological Psychiatry*. August 15, 1993, vol. 34, no. 4, pp. 210–220.

Eastman C.I., Lahmeyer H.W., Watell L.G., Good G.D., Young M.A. "A Placebo-controlled Trial of Light Treatment for Winter Depression," *Journal of Affective Disorders*, 1992, vol. 26, pp. 211–221.

Genhart M., Kelly K.A., Coursey R.D., Datiles M., Rosenthal N.E. "Effects of Bright Light on Mood in Normal Elderly Women," *Psychiatry Research*. 1993, vol. 47, pp. 87–97.

Joffe R.T., Moul D.E., Lam R.W., Levitt A.J., Teicher M.H., Lebegue B., Oren D.A., Buchanan A., Glod C.A., Murray M.G., et al. "Light Visor Treatment for Seasonal Affective Disorder: A Multicenter Study," *Psychiatry Research*. 1993, vol. 46, pp. 29–39.

Krauchi K., Wirz-Justice A., Graw P. "High Intake of Sweets Late in the Day Predicts a Rapid and Persistent Response to Light Therapy in Winter Depression," *Psychiatry Research*. 1993, vol. 46, pp. 107–117.

Lam R.W. "Light Therapy for Seasonal Bulimia" [letter], *American Journal of Psychiatry*. 1989, vol. 146, pp. 1640–1641.

Lam R.W. "Morning Light Therapy for Winter Depression: Predictors of Response," *Acta Psychiatr. Scand*. 1994, vol. 89, pp. 97–101.

Lam R.W., Buchanan A., Mador J.A., Corral M.R. "Hypersomnia and Morning Light Therapy for Winter Depression," *Biol. Psychiatry*. 1992, vol. 31, pp. 1062–1064.

Lam R.W., Buchanan A., Mador J.A., Corral M.R, Remick R.A. "The Effects of Ultraviolet-A Wavelengths in Light Therapy for Seasonal Depression," *Journal of Affective Disorders*. 1992, vol. 24, pp. 237–243.

Levitt, A.J., Joffe R.T., King E. "Dim versus Bright Red (Light-emitting Diode) Light in the Treatment of Seasonal Affective Disorder," *Acta Psychiatrica Scandinavica*. 1994, vol. 89, pp. 341-345.

Levitt A.J., Joffe R.T., Moul D.E., Lam R.W., Teicher M.H., Lebegue B., Murray M.G., Oren D.A., Schwartz P., Buchanan A., Glod C.A., Brown J. "Side Effects of Light Therapy in Seasonal Affective Disorder," *American Journal of Psychiatry*. Vol. 150:4, April 1993, p. 650.

Lewy A.J., Sack R.L., Miller L.S., Hoban T.M. "Anti-depressant and Circadian Phase-shifting Effects of Light," *Science*. 1987, vol. 235, no. 4786, pp. 352-354.

Lewy A.J., Wehr T.A., Goodwin F.K., Newsome D.A., Markey S.P. "Light Suppresses Melatonin Secretion in Humans," *Science*. 1980, vol. 210, no. 4475, pp. 1267-1269.

Norden M.J., Avery D.H. "A Controlled Study of Dawn Simulation in Subsyndromal Winter Depression," *Acta Psychiatrica Scandinavica*. July 1993, vol. 88, no. 1, pp. 67–71.

Oren D.A. et. al. "Treatment of Seasonal Affective Disorder with Green Light and Red Light," *American Journal of Psychiatry*. Vol. 148:4, April 1991, p. 509.

Oren D.A., Jacobsen F.M., Wehr T.A., Cameron C.L., Rosenthal N.E. "Predictors of Response to Phototherapy in Seasonal Affective Disorder," *Comprehensive Psychiatry*. 1992, vol. 33, pp. 111–114.

Ozaki N., Rosenthal N.E., Moul D.E., Schwartz P.J., Oren D.A. "Effects of Phototherapy on Electrooculographic Ratio in Winter Seasonal Affective Disorder," *Psychiatry Research*. 1993, vol. 49, pp. 99–105.

Parry B.L., et al. "Morning Versus Evening Bright Light Treatment of Late Luteal Phase Dysphoric Disorder," *American Journal of Psychiatry*. September 146, vol. 146, p. 9.

Rosenthal N.E., Blehar M.C. *Seasonal Affective Disorders and Phototherapy*. The Guilford Press: New York, 1989.

Rosenthal N.E., Moul D.E., Hellekson C.J., Oren D.A., Frank A., Brainard G.C., Murray M.G., Wehr T.A. "A Multicenter Study of the Light Visor for Seasonal Affective Disorder: No Differences in Efficacy Found Between Two Different Intensities," *Neuropsychopharmacology*. 1993, vol. 8, pp. 151–160.

Rosenthal N.E., Sack D.A., Carpenter C.J., Parry B.L., Mendelson W.B., Wehr T.A. "Anti-depressant Effects of Light in Seasonal Affective Disorder," *American Journal of Psychiatry*. 1985, vol. 142, no. 2, pp. 163-170.

Teicher M.H., Glod C.A., Oren D.A., Luetke C., Schwartz P., Brown C., Rosenthal N.E. "The Phototherapy Light Vistor: There Is More to It Than Meets the Eye." Paper presented at the Society for Light Treatment and Biological Rhythms 4th Annual Conference, Bethesda, Maryland, April 30 and May 1, 1992.

Terman J.S., Terman M., Schlager D., Rafferty B., Rosofsky M., Link M.J., Gallin P.F., Quitkin F.M. "Efficacy of Brief, Intense Light Exposure for Treatment of Winter Depression," *Psychopharmacology Bulletin*. 1990, vol. 26, pp. 3-11.

Terman M., Schlager D.S., Fairhurst S., Perlman B. "Dawn and Dusk Simulation as a Therapeutic Intervention," *Biological Psychiatry*. 1989, vol. 25, pp. 966-970.

Terman M., Schlager D.S. "Twilight Therapeutics, Winter Depression, Melatonin, and Sleep," in *Sleep and Biological Rhythms,* J. Montplaisir and R. Godbout, editors. New York, Oxford University Press. pp. 113-128.

Terman M., Terman J.S. "A Controlled Trial of Light Therapy and Negative Ions," *Society for Light Treatment and Biological Rhythms Abstracts*. 1994, 6:6.

Terman M., Terman J.S., Quitkin F.M., McGrath P.J., Stewart J.W., Rafferty B. "Light Therapy for Seasonal Affective Disorder. A Review of Efficacy," *Neuropsychopharmacology*. 1989, vol. 2, no. 1, pp. 1-22.

Thompson C., Stinson D., Smith A. "Seasonal Affective Disorder and Season-dependent Abnormalities of Melatonin Suppression by Light," *The Lancet*. Vol. 336, Sept. 22, 1990, p. 703.

Wehr T.A., Jacobsen F.M., Sack D.A., Arendt J., Tamarkin L., Rosenthal N.E. "Phototherapy of Seasonal Affective Disorder.

Time of Day and Suppression of Melatonin Are Not Critical for Anti-depressant Effects," *Archives of General Psychiatry.* 1986, vol. 43, no. 9, pp. 870-875.

Wirz-Justice A., Graw P., Krauchi K., Gisin B., Jochum A., Arendt J., Fisch H.U., Buddeberg C., Poldinger W. "Light Therapy in Seasonal Affective Disorder Is Independent of Time of Day or Circadian Phase," *Archives of General Psychiatry.* 1993, vol. 50, no. 12, pp. 929-937.

## Medications

*Compendium of Pharmaceuticals and Specialties: The Canadian Reference for Health Professionals, 1994.* Twenty-ninth edition, Canadian Pharmaceutical Association, Ottawa.

Dilsaver S.C., Qamar A.B., Del Medico V.J. "The Efficacy of Bupropion in Winter Depression: Results of an Open Trial," *Journal of Clinical Psychiatry.* 1992, vol. 53, pp. 252–255.

Julien R.M. *A Primer of Drug Action: A Concise, Nontechnical Guide to the Actions, Uses, and Side Effects of Psychoactive Drugs.* Sixth Edition, W.H. Freeman and Company: New York, 1992.

Winters R.A. *Consumer's Dictionary of Medicines.* Crown Trade Paperbacks: New York, 1993.

## Food and Mood

Berman K., Lam R.W., Goldner E.M. "Eating Attitudes in Seasonal Affective Disorder and Bulimia Nervosa," *Journal of Affective Disorders.* 1993, vol. 29, pp. 219–225.

Ghadirian A.M. "Nutrition and Mental Health: Myth or Reality," *Baha'i Studies Notebook.* 1985, vol. 4, no. 1, 37-46.

Ghadirian A.M., Ananth J., Engelsmann F. "Folic Acid Deficiency and Depression," *Psychosomatics.* 1980, vol. 21, 926-929.

Heller R.F., Heller R.F. *The Carbohydrate Addict's Diet: The Lifelong Solution to Yo-yo Dieting.* Penguin Books: New York, 1991.

Lam R.W., Solyom L., Tompkins A. "Seasonal Mood Symptoms in Bulimia Nervosa and Seasonal Affective Disorder," *Comprehensive Psychiatry.* 1991, vol. 32, pp. 552–558.

Rosenthal N.E., Genhart M.J., Caballero B., Jacobsen F.M., Skwerer R.G., Coursey R.D., Rogers S., Spring B.J.

"Psychobiological Effects of Carbohydrate- and Protein-rich Meals in Patients with Seasonal Affective Disorder and Normal Controls," *Biological Psychiatry*. April 15, 1989, vol. 25, no. 8, pp. 1029–1040.

Wurtman R.J., Wurtman J.J. "Carbohydrates and Depression," *Scientific American*. January 1989, pp. 68–75.

Young S., Ghadirian A.M. "Folic Acid and Psychopathology," *Progress in Neuropsychopharmacology and Biological Psychiatry*. 1989, vol. 3, 841-863.

## The SAD Environment

Albert P.S., Rosen L.N., Alexander J.R., Rosenthal N.E. "The Effect of Daily Variation in Weather and Sleep on Seasonal Affective Disorder," *Psychiatry Research*. 1990, vol. 36, pp. 51–63.

Booker J.M., Hellekson C.J. "Prevalence of Seasonal Affective Disorder in Alaska," *American Journal of Psychiatry*. 1992, vol. 149, pp. 1176–1182.

Eastman C.I. "Natural Summer and Winter Sunlight Exposure Patterns in Seasonal Affective Disorder," *Physiology and Behavior*. November 1990, vol. 48, no. 5, pp. 611–616.

Rosen L.M., Targum S.D., Terman M. et. al. "Prevalence of Seasonal Affective Disorder at Four Latitudes," *Psychiatry Research*. 1990, vol. 31, pp. 131–144.

Savides T.J. "Natural Light Exposure of Young Adults," *Psychology and Behavior*. 1986, vol. 38, pp. 571–574.

# Meal Plans and Recipes

## Meal Plans

The following high-protein and high-carbohydrate meal plans are provided for use in the four-day food and mood trial discussed in Chapter 11. Once you have determined which nutrient group — proteins or carbohydrates — lifts your mood and/or gives you the greatest energy boost, consult a dietician or the National Food Guide to develop a meal plan to meet your total nutritional needs.

## HIGH PROTEIN TWO-DAY MENU

This is a test diet. It does not provide all the nutrients required on a daily basis. If you wish to follow this for more than the two-day test period, consult a registered dietician on how to alter it to meet your total nutrient needs.

| **Breakfast** | 2 boiled eggs |
| | Sliced cheese |
| **Lunch** | *1 bowl chili |
| | *Broiled hamburger patty topped with melted cheese, sliced tomato |
| **Dinner** | *√ California Chicken Casserole |
| | *√ Swiss Steak |
| | Tossed Salad with dressing |

## HIGH CARBOHYDRATE TWO-DAY MENU

This is a test diet. It does not provide all the nutrients required on a daily basis. If you wish to follow this for more than the two-day test period, consult a registered dietician on how to alter it to meet your total nutrient needs.

| **Breakfast** | 1/2 grapefruit |
| | low-fat muffin |
| | fruit-flavored yogurt |
| | 1 orange |
| | cereal with skim milk |
| **Lunch** | √Quesadilla |
| | fresh fruit |
| | *√ English Muffin Pizzas |
| | fresh fruit |
| **Dinner** | *√ Vegetable Lasagna |
| | √ Calzone |
| | carrot & celery sticks |

\* Recipes that can be prepared ahead and frozen. Prepare food in late summer or early fall and freeze in individual or family-sized portions. Only heating will be required. This will be very useful when energy levels are minimal in mid-winter.

√ Recipes contained in this book.

**Notes:**

• Partly skimmed milk can be substituted for skim milk.

• Canned fruit must be packed in fruit juices only.

• Diet yogurt is recommended as it contains less concentrated carbohydrates.

198

# Recipes

The following recipes have been chosen for inclusion in *Don't Be SAD* because they are:

**(1)** easy to prepare when you're low on energy,

**(2)** easy to make in quantity and freeze in advance,

**(3)** low in fat content, or

**(4)** highly recommended by people who are SAD and blue.

**Refer to the number code that appears beside the name of each recipe to determine which of these criteria it satisfies.**

### California Chicken Casserole (2,3)

4–6 chicken pieces

1 large onion

4 stalks celery

3 carrots - sliced

14 oz can tomatoes

> Brown chicken pieces in 2 tsp oil and put into a casserole dish. Sauté onion, celery and carrot slices. Add one can tomatoes. Season with pepper, garlic or thyme. Cover and simmer for 5 minutes. Add 8 oz prepared instant chicken broth. Pour over chicken. Cook at 325°F for one hour. Makes 4 servings.

### Swiss Steak (2,3)

2 pounds round or flank
  steak (½ to ¾" thick)

2 tbsp flour

1 onion - sliced

1 tsp salt (optional)

⅛ tsp pepper

2 ½ cups canned or
  stewed tomatoes

1 tsp Worcestershire sauce

1 tbsp chopped celery

1 tbsp chopped green pepper

> Pound meat on both sides; brown well. Sprinkle both sides with flour and brown lightly again. Brown onion, add salt and pepper. Add remaining ingredients, stir well, add more liquid during cooking if necessary. Cover, cook slowly on top of the stove or in 325°F oven for 1¼ to 1½ hours. Serves 6.

## Quesadilla (1,3)

flour tortilla
canned refried beans
chopped tomato

chopped green onion
shredded mozzarella
salsa

Heat flour tortilla in non-stick frying pan. Spread 2-3 tbsp refried beans over half the tortilla. Sprinkle with chopped tomato and green onion. Sprinkle with 1 tbsp shredded mozzarella cheese. Fold uncovered half of tortilla over the covered half. Flip and heat. Serve with salsa.

## English Muffin Pizzas (1,2,3)

6 English muffins, split
1 6-oz can tomato paste
   or pizza sauce
oregano
garlic powder

*Toppings:*
mushrooms
green peppers
pineapple chunks
onions
1 tsp grated mozzarella cheese per pizza

Arrange muffin halves on ungreased baking sheet. Spread with tomato paste. Sprinkle with spices and toppings, then cheese. (Don't exceed 1 tsp of cheese per pizza. If you do, you'll be adding extra protein.) Freeze to solidify topping sauce, then wrap individual pizzas and return to freezer. Heat unwrapped pizzas in 450°F oven for 12 minutes, in toaster oven, or in covered pan.

## How Much Pasta to Cook?

For a main course pasta dish which includes a number of ingredients along with pasta, I usually plan on about ½ lb/250 g for 4 servings. If it is a dish with only a light sauce such as pesto with pasta I use more. One-half pound/250 g of spaghetti noodles yields about 4 cups when cooked.

The easiest way to measure it is to weigh the uncooked pasta. If you don't have scales you can estimate by dividing the package according to total weight (i.e., divide a 1 lb/500 g package in half to get ½ lb/250 g).

I usually try to cook more pasta than I need and use the extra to make a pasta salad or I mix it with any extra sauce and reheat it for breakfast or lunch.

Reprinted with permission from *The Lighthearted Cookbook.* by Anne Lindsay, published by Key Porter Books Limited, Toronto, Ontario. Copyright © 1988.

## Vegetable Lasagna (2,3)

This is light and easy to make. It can be prepared a day or two in advance and refrigerated.

| | |
|---|---|
| 1 tbsp vegetable oil | 1 tsp each dried basil, oregano |
| 1 small onion, chopped | salt and freshly ground pepper |
| 3 cloves garlic, minced | 3 cups small broccoli florets |
| 1 carrot, chopped | 9 lasagna noodles |
| 1 stalk celery, chopped | 1 cup low-fat cottage cheese |
| 2 cups sliced mushrooms | 3 cups shredded low-fat mozzarella |
| 1 19-oz can tomatoes | cheese |
| 1 7½-oz can tomato sauce | ⅓ cup grated Parmesan cheese |

In a large saucepan, heat oil over medium heat; add onion and cook until tender. Stir in garlic, carrot, celery and mushrooms; cook, stirring often, for 5 minutes.

Add tomatoes, breaking up with fork. Stir in tomato sauce, basil, oregano; season with salt and pepper to taste. Simmer, uncovered, for 10 minutes or until thickened slightly. Let cool; stir in broccoli.

In large pot of boiling water, cook noodles until al dente (tender but firm); drain and rinse under cold water.

In lightly greased 13 x 9 in baking dish, arrange 3 noodles evenly over bottom. Spread with one-half of the vegetable mixture then half of the cottage cheese. Sprinkle with ⅓ of the mozzarella cheese.

Repeat noodle, vegetable mixture, cottage and mozzarella cheese layers once. Arrange remaining noodles over top; sprinkle with remaining mozzarella and Parmesan. Bake in 350°F oven for 35 to 45 minutes or until hot and bubbly. Makes 8 servings.

Reprinted with permission from *The Lighthearted Cookbook.* by Anne Lindsay, published by Key Porter Books Limited, Toronto, Ontario. Copyright © 1988.

201

### Calzone (1,3,4)

frozen bread dough (take
   out of freezer in morning
   to allow this to thaw for
   evening meal)
pizza sauce

*Toppings:*
canned mushrooms
diced tomato
diced onion
canned pineapple
canned artichoke
olives - sliced green or black

Combine a variety of toppings with pizza sauce. Cut thawed bread dough into even pieces (5 or 6). Flatten bread dough with rolling pin. Put about ¼ cup of topping sauce mixture on flattened bread dough. Fold dough over top of filling to form a turnover. Place in preheated oven (350°F) and bake for 15–20 minutes. Leftover calzones can be eaten cold or reheated for the next day's lunch.

### Easy Oven Beef and Vegetable Stew (2,3)

1 ½ lb stewing beef
¼ cup all-purpose flour
6 small onions
2 large potatoes,
   cut into small chunks
3 large carrots, cut in chunks
3 cloves garlic, minced
2 cups diced turnip
3 cups water

1 ½ cups beef stock or bouillon
1 7 ½-oz can tomato sauce
1 tsp dried thyme
½ tsp dried oregano
¼ tsp freshly ground pepper
1 bay leaf
½ tsp grated orange rind
   (optional)

Remove all visible fat from beef, cut into 1-inch cubes. In large casserole or Dutch oven, toss beef with flour. Add onion, potatoes, carrots, garlic, turnip, water, beef stock, tomato sauce, thyme, oregano, pepper, bay leaf and orange rind; stir to mix.

Bake, covered, in 325°F oven for 3 hours, stirring occasionally (if you can remember to). Remove bay leaf. Makes 8 servings.

Reprinted with permission from *The Lighthearted Cookbook*. by Anne Lindsay, published by Key Porter Books Limited, Toronto, Ontario. Copyright © 1988.

## Family Favourite Shepherd's Pie
## (2 - meat portion only, 3)

| | |
|---|---|
| 1 lb lean ground beef, pork or lamb | ⅓ cup tomato paste |
| 2 onions chopped | ⅔ cup water |
| 2 cloves garlic, minced | 1 tsp dried thyme |
| 1 carrot, minced (optional) | 2 tsp Worcestershire sauce |
| 2 cups mashed potato (about 5 medium potatoes) | freshly ground pepper |
| | paprika |

In skillet over medium heat, cook beef, stirring to break up meat, until brown; pour off fat. Add onions, garlic and carrot (if using); cook until tender. Add tomato paste, water, thyme, Worcestershire sauce, and pepper to taste. Simmer for 5 minutes, stirring up any brown bits on bottom of pan.

Spoon meat mixture into 8-cup baking or microwave-safe dish; spread mashed potatoes evenly on top. Sprinkle with paprika to taste. Bake in 375°F oven for 35 minutes or until heated through, or microwave at high (100%) power for 9 minutes. Makes 5 servings.

Reprinted with permission from *The Lighthearted Cookbook*. by Anne Lindsay, published by Key Porter Books Limited, Toronto, Ontario. Copyright © 1988.

## Bev's Best Stir Fry (1,3)

*Stir Fry*

1 lb beef sirloin, boneless
   chicken breasts, or
   pork tenderloin,
   thinly sliced
8 cups sliced, mixed
   vegetables (e.g. carrots,
   broccoli, mushrooms, onion,
   cauliflower, green pepper)
OR 2 pkgs commercial stir-fry vegetables

*Sauce*

1 cup chicken stock
2 tbsp oyster sauce
2 tsp granulated sugar
¼ tsp ginger, ground
¼ tsp garlic powder

Spray wok or frying pan with vegetable oil spray. Brown meat. Mix sauce ingredients in bowl. Add vegetables and sauce. Stir fry for about 6 minutes. Serve with rice or noodles. Makes 6 servings.

## Bean and Pasta Soup (1,3)

2 tsp vegetable oil
1 medium onion, chopped
¼ tsp garlic powder
1 can kidney beans, drained
1 or 2 carrots, thinly sliced
1 stalk celery

1 19-oz can tomatoes
1 beef bouillon cube
½ cup elbow macaroni
1 ½ cups water
½ tsp basil

Sauté onion in oil, add garlic powder. Add kidney beans, carrot, celery, canned tomatoes, bouillon cube, water and basil. Break canned tomatoes up with a fork. Cover and simmer for 30 minutes. Add macaroni and continue to cook uncovered for about 10 minutes. Salt and pepper to taste. Serves 3 to 4.

## Three-Day Coleslaw (3)

Once prepared, this tasty salad can be used as a side dish for up to three days if kept in the refrigerator.

¼ cup white vinegar
2 tbsp vegetable oil
½ tsp salt
¼ tsp celery seed
1 tsp dry mustard
2 tbsp granulated sugar

6 cups chopped cabbage
½ cup chopped green pepper
½ cup grated carrot
½ cup minced onion

In a saucepan, bring vinegar, oil, salt, celery seed, dry mustard and sugar to a boil. Remove from heat. Combine vegetables in a bowl. Pour dressing over salad and toss well. Cover and refrigerate.

## Chicken Fajitas (1,3)

8 flour tortillas
salsa
2 tbsp fresh cilantro,
    chopped (optional)

*Filling:*
4 boneless chicken breasts,
    skinned and thinly sliced
1 onion, sliced
1 green pepper, sliced
2 garlic cloves, crushed
2 tsp chili powder
2 tsp cumin

Warm tortillas by wrapping all 8 in a damp tea towel and microwaving or by heating tortillas individually in a non-stick frying pan and setting them aside in a stack covered with a tea towel. Sauté filling ingredients over medium heat in frying pan prepared with vegetable oil spray. When chicken is cooked through, remove from heat. Divide filling among the 8 tortillas, sprinkle with cilantro, then wrap them up. Use salsa as an accompaniment at the table. Serves 3 to 4.

### Buttermilk, Bran & Blueberry Muffins (2,3)

3 cups natural bran

2 cups whole wheat flour

½ cup granulated sugar

1 tbsp baking powder

1 tsp baking soda

2 eggs, beaten

2 cups buttermilk

⅓ cup vegetable oil

½ cup molasses

1 cup fresh or frozen blueberries

In a large bowl, mix together bran, flour, sugar, baking powder and baking soda. In another bowl, combine eggs, buttermilk, oil and molasses; pour into bran mixture and stir just enough to moisten, being careful not to overmix. Fold in blueberries.

Spoon into nonstick or paper-lined large muffin tins, filling almost to top. Bake in 375°F oven for about 25 minutes or until firm to touch. Remove from oven and let stand for two minutes before removing muffins from tin. Makes about 20 muffins.

1 muffin = 5g fat (equal to 1 tsp)

Reprinted with permission from *The Lighthearted Cookbook*. by Anne Lindsay, published by Key Porter Books Limited, Toronto, Ontario. Copyright © 1988.

### Broccoli Salad (1,4)

1 bunch of broccoli, finely chopped

1 onion, finely chopped

½ cup sunflower seeds

1 cup raisins (chop coarsely if they are big plump ones)

1 lb bacon (cook, remove fat then chop)

Mix above ingredients. Add following dressing just before serving.

**Dressing**

1 tbsp cider vinegar     ½ cup sugar

½ cup mayonnaise

## Nancy's Potato Soup (2 - up to *, 4)

2 cups chopped onion

1 cup chopped celery

2 tbsp oil or use
   vegetable oil spray

1 cup chopped carrot

4 cups finely chopped potato

2 tbsp chopped parsley

1 tsp salt

¼ tsp pepper

⅛ tsp paprika

2 cups chicken bouillon

1 cup light sour cream

chives

grated low-fat cheddar cheese
   (optional)

Saute onion and celery in oil or a pan covered with vegetable oil spray until onion is transparent. Simmer carrot, potato, parsley, salt, pepper, paprika and chicken bouillon until potatoes are tender (about 20 minutes). Add water if necessary. Slightly puree cooked vegetable mixture.* Add sour cream and heat without boiling. Garnish with chives and grated cheddar cheese.

Adapted from Alberta Potato Producers recipe.

## Bean Salad (1,3,4)

1 can green beans

1 can yellow beans

1 can kidney beans

Pinch of garlic salt

2 tsp parsley

1 tbsp white sugar

½ tsp pepper

½ tsp dry mustard

2 tbsp vinegar

1 tbsp oil

Drain beans and pour into serving dish. Mix the remaining ingredients and pour over beans. Let the mixture marinate for 3 to 4 hours. Slices of Spanish onion and celery may be added before serving.

## Oatmeal Carrot Muffins (2,3)

| | |
|---|---|
| 1 cup buttermilk | 1 cup all purpose flour |
| 1 cup quick cooking rolled oats | ¼ cup granulated sugar |
| ½ cup grated carrots | 1 tbsp baking powder |
| ¼ cup packed brown sugar | 1 tsp salt |
| ¼ cup melted margarine | ½ tsp baking soda |
| 1 egg slightly beaten | ¾ cup raisins (optional) |
| 1 tsp grated orange rind | |

In a large bowl, pour buttermilk over oats; stir to mix. Cover and let stand for 2 hours or refrigerate overnight. Mix together carrots, brown sugar, margarine, egg and orange rind; stir into oat mixture. Sift together flour, granulated sugar, baking powder, salt and baking soda; stir in raisins (if used). Stir batter until just moistened.

Spoon into nonstick or paper-lined large muffin tins, filling almost to top. Bake in 400°F oven 20-25 minutes or until firm to touch. Let stand for two minutes before removing from tins. Makes 12 muffins.

1 muffin = 5g fat (or the equivalent of 1 tsp).

*Note: Many grocery stores now sell low-fat muffins.*

Reprinted with permission from *The Lighthearted Cookbook.* by Anne Lindsay, published by Key Porter Books Limited, Toronto, Ontario. Copyright © 1988.

## Wonderful Tomato Soup (1,3,4)

3 ½ cups canned tomatoes
and juice
½ small onion
2 cups water
2 tsp sugar

1 ½ tsp seasoned salt
Dash of pepper
2 tbsp soft butter
2 tbsp flour

In covered container, blend tomatoes at low speed until lique-
fied. Pour into a saucepan. Blend remaining ingredients until smooth. Add to the tomatoes; simmer for 20 minutes.
Garnish with chopped green pepper, cheese or parsley. Serves
4 to 6.

**Tomato Plus Soup:** To above, add vegetables, pasta,
chicken, sliced frankfurters and/or tiny meatballs.

This recipe is wonderfully quick. It also lends itself well
to crock pot cookery. Start the basic soup simmering in your
crock pot in the morning, then add any extras 10-15 minutes
before serving.

## Stackee-Upees (1,4)

Place each of the following ingredients in a separate serving bowl on
the table and let everyone construct their own layered meal. The amount
of each ingredient will vary depending on the number of people being
served. This recipe serves 8.

Chow mein noodles
4 cups cooked rice
2 cups chicken, cooked and diced
Gravy (mix 1 can each: cream of
mushroom soup, cream of
chicken soup and chicken broth)
1 cup hot peas
1 cup sliced celery
½ cup green onions, thinly sliced

1 to 2 cups cheddar cheese, grated
1 20-oz can pineapple chunks,
drained
½ cup shredded, unsweetened
coconut
½ cup slivered almonds
3 medium tomatoes, diced
½ cup green pepper, diced
Parsley, coarsely chopped

# APPENDIX C

# SAD Clinics and Practitioners

The following list includes clinics in which light therapy studies are being conducted and medical practices offering treatment for SAD. Although we have made every effort to be as thorough as possible, it is by no means a comprehensive list. Consult your doctor to determine the facility closest to you that can provide the most appropriate treatment to meet your specific needs. We cannot take responsibility for any outcome of consulting the listed individuals and programs.

## UNITED STATES

### Alaska

**Dr. Gregory J. Hanebuth**
3310 Max Circle #1
Anchorage, AK 99507
**Dr. Bruce Smith**
8550 Denali Street., Suite 1306
Anchorage, AK 99503
(907) 272-4741
**Dr. Aaron Wolf**
4001 Dale Street, Suite 101
Anchorage, AK 99504
(907) 561-1361

### Arkansas

**Dr. Frederick Guggenheim**
Department of Psychiatry
University of Arkansas for Medical
    Sciences
4301 West Markham, Slot 554
Little Rock, AR 72205
(501) 686-5816

### California

*La Jolla-San Diego*
**Dr. Daniel F. Kripke**
Department of Psychiatry

University of California at San Diego
Circadian Pacemaker Laboratory
Box 0667, 9500 Gilman Drive
La Jolla, CA 92093-0667
(619) 534-7131
**Dr. Barbara L. Parry**
Department of Psychiatry
University of California at San Diego
Box 0804
La Jolla, CA 92093
(619) 543-5592

*Los Angeles Area*
**Center for Mood Disorders**
12301 Wilshire Blvd., Suite 210
Los Angeles, CA 90025
(213) 207-8448
**Dr. John P. Docherty**
National Medical Enterprises
2700 Colorado Avenue
Santa Monica, CA 90404
(310) 998-6739
**Dr. Robert H. Gerner**
1990 South Bundy Drive, #790
Los Angeles, CA 90025
(310) 206-8448

**Dr. Michael J. Gitlin**
300 UCLA Medical Plaza, #2200
Los Angeles, CA 90024
(310) 206-5133
**Dr. David A. Sack**
College Hospital
10802 College Place
Cerritos, CA 90701
(310) 924-3116

## Colorado

**Dr. R. Timothy Pollack**
Health Enhancement Center, Inc.
8370 West Coal Mine Avenue
Suite 107
Littleton, CO 80123
(303) 972-0714

## Connecticut

**Dr. Francine C. Howland**
45 Trumbull Street
New Haven, CT 06510
(203) 624-3516
**Dr. Neil Liebowitz**
Connecticut Anxiety & Depression
    Treatment Center
1031 Farmington Ave.
Farmington, CT 06032
(203) 677-2550
**Dr. Charles S. Mirabile**
Box 683, Upper Main Street
Sharon, CT 06069
(203) 364-0740
**Dr. Daniel Romanoes**
Torrington Office Plaza, Suite 301
Torrington, CT 06790
(203) 482-9321
**Dr. Alan J. Sholomskas**
2 Whitney Ave., Suite 2004
New Haven, CT 06510
(203) 776-2077

## D.C. Metropolitan Area

**Dr. Frederick M. Jacobsen**
Transcultural Mental Health Institute
1301 - 20th Street N.W., #711
Washington, D.C. 20036
(202) 234-1742

## Florida

**Dr. Siong-Chi Lin**
Mayo Clinic, Sleep Center
4500 San Pablo Road
Jacksonville, FL 32224
(904) 223-2039
**Dr. Donald L. Sherry**
3300 S.W. 34th Avenue, #140
Ocala, FL 34474-7427
(904) 854-7700
**Dr. Robert G. Skwerer**
635 South Orange Avenue, Suite 7
Sarasota, FL 34236-7503
(813) 954-0911

## Georgia

**Dr. George Johnson**
682 Lanier Drive
Gainesville, GA 30505
(404) 532-5640
**Dr. Charles Melville**
25-B Lenox Pointe, N.E.
Atlanta, GA 30324
(404) 266-8881
**Dr. Charles B. Nemeroff**
Department of Psychiatry and
    Behavioral Sciences
Emory Univ. School of Medicine
Box AF
Atlanta, GA 30322
(404) 727-8382

## Hawaii

**Dr. Enrico G. Camara**
Department of Psychiatry
University of Hawaii
1356 Lusitana Street, 4th Floor
Honolulu, HI 06813
(808) 247-2191

## Idaho

**Dr. Winslow R. Hunt**
155 South Second Avenue
Pocatello, ID 83201
(208) 232-3423

## Illinois

**Dr. Charmane I. Eastman**
Biological Rhythms Research
    Laboratory
Rush Presbyterian-St. Luke's
    Medical Center
1653 West Congress Parkway
Chicago, IL 60612
(312) 942-8328
**Dr. Henry Lahmeyer**
University of Illinois
801 South Morgan
Box 4348
Chicago, IL 60680
**Dr. Richard H. Spector**
2850 West 95th Street, Suite 208
Evergreen Park, IL 60642
(708) 424-2024
**Dr. Michael Young**
Biological Rhythms Research
    Laboratory
Rush Presbyterian-St. Luke's
    Medical Center
1653 West Congress Parkway
Chicago, IL 60612
(312) 942-8328

## Indiana

**Dr. John Nurnberger**
Professor of Psychiatry
The Institute of Psychiatric Research
791 Union Drive
Indiana University Medical Center
Indianapolis, IN
(317) 274-8382
**Dr. Richard H. Spector**
833 West Lincoln Highway, Suite 400
Schererville, IN 46375
(219) 322-5662

## Iowa

**Dr. Bruce Pfohl**
University of Iowa Hospitals & Clinics
Department of Psychiatry
200 Hawkins Drive
Iowa City, IA 52242
(319) 356-1350

## Kentucky

**Dr. B. Kishore Gupta**
Department of Psychiatry
University of Louisville
133 Chenoweth Lane
Louisville, KY 40207
(502) 895-6368

## Louisiana

**Department of Psychiatry**
Louisiana State University
Medical School
Box 33932
Shreveport, LA 71130
(318) 674-6042

## Maryland
### Baltimore

**The Affective Disorders Clinic**
John Hopkins University School of
    Medicine
Meyer 3-181
Baltimore, MD 21287-7381
(301) 955-3246

**Dr. J. Raymond de Paulo, Jr.**
Department of Psychiatry
John Hopkins University School of
    Medicine
Meyer 3-181
Baltimore, MD 21287-7381
(301) 955-3246

**Dr. David Roth**
Shepard Pratt Hospital
6501 North Charles Street
Baltimore, MD 21285-6815
(410) 938-3000 ext. 4219

## Bethesda

**Dr. Dan A. Oren**
5612 Shields Drive
Bethesda, MD 20817
(301) 231-4410

**Dr. Norman E. Rosenthal**
Seasonal Studies Program
National Institute of Mental Health
Building 10, Room 4S-239
9000 Rockville Pike
Bethesda, MD 20892
(301) 496-2141

**Dr. Thomas A. Wehr**
National Institute of Mental Health
Building 10, Room 4S-239
9000 Rockville Pike
Bethesda, MD 20892
(301) 530-7336

# Massachusetts

## Amherst

**Dr. Bruce Goderez**
33 School Street
Springfield, MA 01105
(413) 739-7766

**Dr. Benjamin Levy**
University Health Services
University of Massachusetts

14 Amherst Road, RFD#3
Amherst, MA 01003
(413) 545-2337

## Boston Area

**Dr. Janis L. Anderson**
Seasonal Affective Disorder Clinic
Brigham and Women's Hospital
211 Longwood Avenue
Boston, MA 02115
(617) 732-7993

**Carol A. Glod**
Hall Mercer Building
McLean Hospital
115 Mill Street
Belmont, MA 02178
(617) 855-2476

**Dr. Dermott O'Rouke**
C-R-C-M-I-T
Massachusetts General Hospital
40 Ames Street
Cambridge, MA 02142
(617) 253-3091

**Dr. Gary S. Sachs**
Massachusetts General Hospital
15 Parkman Street, ACC-715
Boston, MA 02114
(617) 726-3488

**Dr. Martin H. Teicher**
Hall Mercer Building
McLean Hospital
115 Mill Street
Belmont, MA 02178
(617) 855-2970

# Michigan

**Dr. Oliver G. Cameron**
University of Michigan
Riverview Building
900 Wall Street, J232
Ann Arbor, MI 48109-0722
(313) 764-0267

**Dr. Mark Demitrack**
University of Michigan Hospitals
UH 8D, Box 0116
Ann Arbor, MI 48109
(313) 936-4860

**Dr. Pat Guilford**
Borgess Medical Services
1722 Shaffer Street
Kalamazoo, MI 49001-1643
(616) 349-4460

**Dr. D. Lynn Hughes**
3800 Heritage Avenue
Okemos, MI 48864
(517) 347-4848

**Juan Lopez**
Mental Health Research Institute
Box 0720
Ann Arbor, MI 48109
(313) 633-3141

**Dr. Elizabeth Young**
Mood Disorders Program
Department of Psychiatry
University of Michigan Hospitals
1500 East Medical Center Drive
Ann Arbor, MI 48109
(313) 936-2087

## Minnesota

**Dr. Paul A. Arbisi**
Minneapolis Veterans Medical Center
One Veterans Drive
Minneapolis, MN 55417
(612) 725-2074

**Michael De Sanctis, PhD, ABPP**
Health Renewal Center
Psychology Consultants
Gallery Professional Building
17 Exchange Street West, Suite 750
St. Paul, MN 55102-1036
(612) 232-4120

**Dr. Frederick Engstrum**
Mental Health Department
5000 West 39th Street
Minneapolis, MN 55416
(612) 927-3371

**Dr. Sandra C. Reese**
Family Counseling
2025 Stearns Way
St. Cloud, MN 56303
(612) 255-2041

## Missouri

**Dr. Dale J. Anderson**
12520 Olive Blvd.
St. Louis, MO 63141
(314) 576-6692

## Montana

**Dr. Michael J. Silverglat**
554 West Broadway
Missoula, MT 59802
(406) 721-6050

## Nebraska

**Dr. Robert G. Osborne**
2221 South 17th Street, Suite 110
Lincoln, NE 68502
(402) 476-7557

**Dr. Kay M. Shilling**
7602 Pacific Street, Suite 302
Omaha, NE 68114
(402) 393-4355

## New Hampshire

**Dr. James R. Antisdel**
40 Bay Street
Manchester, NH 03104
(603) 924-7236

**Dr. James M. Claiborn**
80 Palomino Lane, Suite 203
Bedford, NH 03110
(603) 624-2272

**Dr. John Docherty**
Nashua Brookside Hospital
11 Northwest Blvd.
Nashua, NH 03063
(603) 886-5000
**Dr. A. Frank**
North East Psychiatric Associates
14 Celina Avenue, P.O. Box 6010
Nashua, NH 03063-6010
(603) 595-0601
**Manadnock Family Services**
454 Old Street Road, Suite #303
Peterborough, NH 03458
(603) 924-7236
**Dr. C. Louis Ravaris**
Dartmouth Medical Center
One Medical Center Drive
Lebanon, NH 03766
(603) 650-5805
**Dr. Janet R. Wakefield**
White Mountain Mental Health
     Center
Box 559
Littleton, NH 03561
(603) 444-5358

### New Jersey

**Dr. Jeffrey T. Apter**
Princeton Psychiatric Centers
330 North Harrison Street, Suite 6
Princeton, NJ 08540
(609) 921-3555
**Dr. Robert K. Davies**
47 Maple Street
Summit, NJ 07901
(908) 277-1010

**Dr. Robert Moreines**
**Dr. Stuart Kushne**
Warren Commons
5 Mountain Blvd., Suite 6
Warren, NJ 07060
(908) 753-4444
**Dr. Benjamin Natelson**
Department of Neurosciences
New Jersey Medical School
185 South Orange Avenue
Newark, NJ 07103
(201) 982-5208
**Dr. Steven Resnick**
Suite 162, CN 5256
Princeton, NJ 08543
(609) 683-1531
**Dr. Naomi Vilko**
Princeton Health Care Center
419 North Harrison Street, Suite 206
Princeton, NJ 08540
(609) 924-3225

### New York
### *New York City & Long Island*

**Dr. Richard P. Brown**
30 East End Avenue
New York, NY 10028
(212) 737-0821
**Dr. Minna R. Fyer**
New York Hospital
Payne-Whitney Clinic
525 East 68th Street
New York, NY 10021-4873
**Dr. Lauren Gorman**
15 West 81st Street
New York, NY 10024
(212) 548-0568

215

**Dr. Julie A. Hatterer**
11 East 68th Street
New York, NY 10021-4955
(212) 472-0889
**Dr. Henry L. McCurtis**
146 Central Park West
New York, NY 10023
(212) 580-2222
and
Department of Psychiatry
Harlem Hospital
506 Lennox Avenue
New York, NY 10037
(212) 939-3060
**Dr. Leslie L. Powers**
15 West 75th Street, Suite 4B
New York, NY 10023
(212) 724-5222
**Dr. David S. Schlager**
State University of New York at
    Stony Brook
HSC T10, Room 020
Stony Brook, NY 11794-8101
(516) 444-1004
**Dr. Norman Sussman**
Department of Psychiatry
New York University Medical
    Center
550 - 1st Avenue
New York, NY 10016
(212) 737-7946
**Dr. Michael Terman**
Winter Depression Program
Columbia-Presbyterian Medical
    Center
722 West 168th Street, Box 50
New York, NY 10032
(212) 960-5712

### Rochester

**Dr. Michael R. Privitera**
Mood Disorders Center
Department of Psychiatry
Univ. of Rochester Medical Center
Brighton Campus Park
2024 West Henrietta Road, Suite 6C
Rochester, NY 14623
(716) 475-0440
**Dr. Mildred D. Rust**
1360 Monroe Avenue
Rochester, NY 14618
(716) 442-9601 ext. 7

### Rockland County

**Dr. James W. Flax**
11 Medical Park Drive, Suite 102
Pomona, NY 10970
(914) 362-2557

### Syracuse Area

**Dr. Richard Kavey**
R.R. #2, 2922 Eager Road
Lafayette, NY 13084
(315) 677-3486

### Westchester County

**Dr. Joseph Deltito**
New York Hospital-Cornell
    University Medical Center
Anxiety and Mood Disorders Program
21 Bloomingdale Road
White Plains, NY 10605
(914) 997-5967
**Dr. Mohamed Yahia**
Inpatient Admission Units
FDR Veterans Administration
    Medical Center
Chappaqua, NY 10548
(914) 238-3546

## North Carolina

**Dr. Dan G. Blazer**
Box 3005
Duke University School of Medicine
Durham, NC 27710
(919) 684-4128

**Dr. Jack D. Edinger**
Ambulatory Sleep Laboratory
Box 2908
Duke University Medical Center
Durham, NC 27710
(919) 681-8725

**Dr. Michael A. Hill**
Univ. of North Carolina Hospitals
C.B. 7160
Chapel Hill, NC 27599-7160
(919) 966-3376

**Dr. Gail Marsh**
Box 2908
Duke University Medical Center
Durham, NC 27710-0000
(919) 681-8777

**Dr. William Simmons**
932 Hendersonville Road
Forest Center, #101
Asheville, NC 28803
(704) 274-1415

## North Dakota

**Dr. Robert Olson**
700 - 1st Avenue South
Fargo, ND 58103
(701) 234-4093

## Ohio

### Cleveland

**Dr. Ruth Ragucci**
11201 Shaker Blvd., #204
Cleveland, OH 44104
(216) 721-6770

### Dayton

**Dr. Gregory G. Young**
1745 Big Hill Road
Dayton, OH 45439
(513) 293-2507

### Columbus

**Donna Gray Boyd**
5174 Blazer Memorial Parkway
Dublin, OH 43017
(614) 761-3303

**Dr. Robert W. Clark**
POB 1, Suite 206
5975 East Broad Street
Columbus, OH 43213

**Dr. Hissako Koizumi**
Harding Outpatient Clinic
1925 Dublin-Granville Road
Columbus, OH 43229
(614) 848-9900

**Dr. L. Edgar Lee**
Wesley Health Center - RMH
3535 Olentangy River Road
Columbus, OH 43214
(614) 566-4710

**Dr. Daniel J. Martin**
OSU Clinics - Adult Psychiatry
473 West 12th Avenue
Columbus, OH 43210
(614) 293-8050

**Dr. Stephen Stern**
OSU Outpatient Clinics, Adult
    Psychiatry
456 West 10th Avenue, 2B
Columbus, OH 43210
(614) 293-8050

## Oklahoma

**Dr. David P. Crass**
1725 East 19th Street, Suite 604
Tulsa, OK 74104
(918) 743-6694

## Oregon

Dr. George C.D. Kjaer
132 East Broadway, Suite 303
Eugene, OR 97401
(503) 686-2027
Dr. Alfred J. Lewy
Dr. Robert L. Sack
Dr. Clifford M. Singer
Sleep and Mood Disorders
    Laboratory
Department of Psychiatry
University of Oregon Health
    Sciences Center
3181 S.W. Sam Jackson Park Road
Portland, OR 97201
(503) 494-5635

## Pennsylvania

### Philadelphia

Dr. George C. Brainard
Department of Neurology
Jefferson Medical College
1025 Walnut Street
Philadelphia, PA 19107
(215) 955-7644
Dr. Brenda Byrne
Clorinda G. Margolis and Associates
1015 Chestnut Street, #1500
Philadelphia, PA 19107
(215) 592-8165
Dr. Karl Doghramji
Sleep Disorder Center
1015 Walnut Street, Suite 327-D
Philadelphia, PA 19107
Dr. William Sonis
Philadelphia Child Guidance Clinic
2 Children's Center
Philadelphia, PA 19104

### Pittsburgh

Dr. Edward Friedman
University of Pittsburgh
School of Medicine
3811 O'Hara Street
Pittsburgh, PA 15241
(412) 383-1210
Dr. Michael Thase
University of Pittsburgh
School of Medicine
3811 O'Hara Street
Pittsburgh, PA 15213
(412) 383-1200

### Other

Dr. Leroy J. Pelicci
748 Quincy Avenue
Scranton, PA 18510
(717) 342-8633

## Rhode Island

Dr. Mark S. Bauer
Department of Psychiatry and
    Human Behavior
Brown University
Box G-VAH/ 116A2
Providence, RI 02912
(401) 457-3333

## South Carolina

Dr. Timothy D. Brewston
Institute of Psychiatry
Medical University of South
    Carolina
171 Ashley Avenue
Charleston, SC 29425-0742
(803) 792-7183

## Tennessee

**Dr. Kenneth O. Jobson**
Tennessee Psychiatry and
    Psychopharmacology Clinic
9401 Park West Boulevard
Knoxville, TN 37923
(615) 690-8190
**Department of Psychiatry**
James H. Quillen College of
    Medicine
Box 70654
East Tennessee State University
Johnson City, TN 37614
(214) 692-9660

## Texas

### Dallas

**Dr. Philip Becker**
**Dr. Andrew Jamieson**
Sleep Medicine Institute
Presbyterian Hospital of Dallas
8200 Walnut Hill Lane
Dallas, TX 75231
(214) 696-8563
**Dr. John W. Cain**
**Dr. A. John Rush**
Department of Psychiatry
University of Texas Southwestern
5323 Harry Hines Blvd.
Dallas, TX 75235-8898
(214) 648-3888
**Dr. Howard Roffwarg**
8226 Douglas, #616
Dallas, TX 75240
(214) 692-9660

### El Paso

**Dr. Jean R. Joseph-Vanderpool**
600 Sunland Park Drive
Building 6, #100
El Paso, TX 79912
(915) 833-5855

### Houston

**Dr. Stuart C. Yudofsky**
Professor and Chairman
Department of Psychiatry
Baylor College of Medicine
1 Baylor Plaza
Houston, TX 77030
(713) 798-4945

### Other

**Dr. Cynthia Desmond**
c/o Desart Hills
4201 Texas Avenue South
College Station, TX 77840
(409) 846-4592

## Utah

**Dr. Joanne L. Brown**
Cottonwood Counseling Center
525 East 4500 South, Suite F200
Salt Lake City, UT 84107
(801) 266-6413
**Dr. William Byerly**
Department of Psychiatry
University Medical Center
50 North Medical Drive
Salt Lake City, UT 84152

## Vermont

**Dr. Ray C. Abney**
Rt. 30 Brattleboro Professional
    Center
P.O. Box 1616
Brattleboro, VT 05302
(802) 257-2442

Dr. Stephen M. Cohen
118 Pine Street
Burlington, VT 05401
(802) 864-5280
Dr. John R. Edwards
118 Pine Street
Burlington, VT 05401
(802) 658-2762
Dr. Edward A. Mueller
Rutland Area Community Services
78 South Main Street
Rutland, VT 05701
(802) 775-2381

## Virginia
Dr. Tobin Jones
1600 East Little Creek Road, #346
Norfolk, VA 23518
(804) 441-1717

## Washington
Dr. David H. Avery
Harborview Medical Center, ZA-99
325 - 9th Avenue
Seattle, WA 98104
(206) 223-3425
Dr. Carla Hellekson
Group Health Hospital - ESMH
2700 - 152 Avenue NE
Redmond, WA 98052
(206) 883-5320
Dr. Michael Norden
10740 Meridian Avenue North,
    Suite 101
Seattle, WA 98133
(206) 361-7696
Dr. Keith L. Rogers
Psychiatry Services
#116A, 1660 South Columbian Way
Seattle, WA 98108
(206) 764-2063

## Wisconsin
Dr. Nancy Barklage
Dr. Stephen J. Weiler
Dr. Ruth Benca
Center for Affective Disorders
Department of Psychiatry
University of Wisconsin Hospital
    and Clinics
600 Highland Drive
Madison, WI 53792
(608) 263-6092
Dr. Jan van Schaik
1120 Dewey Avenue
Wauwatosa, WI 53213
(414) 258-2600

# CANADA

## Alberta
### *Calgary*
Leslie Demytruk
Crisis Management Resources
Suite 600, 250 - 6th Avenue SW
Calgary, AB T2P 3H7
(403) 263-2200
Dr. Chris Gorman
Foothills Hospital, Mood Disorder
    Clinic
1403 - 29th Street NW
Calgary, AB T2N 2T9
(403) 270-8222
Dr. Adam Moscovitch
#300, 295 Midpark Way SE
Calgary, AB T2X 2A8
(403) 254-6400
Dr. Robin T. Reesal
Calgary General Hospital
841 Centre Ave.
Calgary, AB T2E 0A1
(403) 268-9121

### Edmonton

**Dr. Carl A. Blashko**
27, Cedars Professional Park
2923 - 66th Street
Edmonton, AB T6K 4C1
(403) 461-4794

**Dr. Yakov Shapiro**
Cedars Professional Park
2931 - 66th Street
Edmonton, AB T6K 4C1
(403) 490-1014

## British Columbia

**Dr. B. Bright**
#103, 11743 - 224th Street
Maple Ridge, BC V2X 6A4
(604) 467-2041

**Dr. John Hallonquist**
Psychology Department
University of the Cariboo
P.O. Box 3010
Kamloops, BC V2C 5N3
(604) 828-5314

**Dr. Raymond W. Lam**
Department of Psychiatry
University of British Columbia
2255 Wesbrook Mall
Vancouver, BC V6T 2A1
(604) 822-7325

**Dr. Joseph A. Mador**
1211 West 8th Avenue
Vancouver, BC V6H 1C7
(604) 734-2553

**Dr. H.E. Soufi**
Head, Department of Psychiatry
Ridge Meadows Hospital
Maple Ridge, BC V2X 7G5
(604) 463-4111 ext. 356

## Manitoba

**Eden Mental Health Centre**
1500 Pembina Avenue
Winkler, MB R6W 1T4
(204) 325-4325

**Health Sciences Centre**
Outpatient Psychiatry Department
697 McDermot Avenue
Winnipeg, MB R3A 1R9
(204) 787-3367

**Dr. Mark Lander**
Mood Disorders Unit
PZ 202 - PsycHealth Centre
771 Bannatyne Avenue
Winnipeg, MB R3E 3N4
(204) 787-7078

## Nova Scotia

**Dr. C. Charles Mate-Kole**
Department of Psychology
Dalhousie University
Halifax, NS B3H 4G1
(902) 494-1580

**Dr. Max Michalon**
Department of Psychiatry
Camp Hill Medical Centre
Abbie J. Lane Building
1763 Robie Street
Halifax, NS B3H 3G2
(902) 496-2125

**Dr. Rachel L. Morehouse**
Sleep Disorders Laboratory
Camp Hill Medical Centre
Abbie J. Lane Building
4th Floor, 1763 Robie Street
Halifax, NS B3H 3G2
(902) 496-4298

221

## Ontario

### Toronto

**Dr. Vincent DeMarco**
Humber Memorial Hospital
200 Church Street
Weston, ON M9N 1N8
(416) 243-4458

**Dr. Kristin Gisladottir**
203, 2425 Bloor Street West
Toronto, ON M6S 4W4
(416) 762-1119

**Dr. Sidney Kennedy**
Clarke Institute of Psychiatry
250 College Street
Toronto, ON M5T 1R8
(416) 979-6868

**Dr. Jeffrey J. Lipsitz**
Sleep Disorders Centre of
    Metropolitan Toronto
2888 Bathurst Street, First Floor
Toronto, ON M6B 4H6
(416) 785-1128

**Dr. Harvey Moldofsky**
Toronto Hospital, Western Division
Department of Psychiatry
399 Bathurst Street
Toronto, ON M5T 2S8
(416) 369-5109

**Dr. Colin M. Shapiro**
Toronto Hospital, Western Division
Department of Psychiatry
399 Bathurst Street
Toronto, ON M5T 2S8

### Hamilton

**Dr. Richard G. Guscott**
Hamilton Psychiatric Hospital
100 West 5th Street, P.O. Box 585
Hamilton, ON L8N 3K7
(905) 575-6014

**Dr. Russell T. Joffee**
Hamilton Psychiatric Hospital
c/o Mood Disorder Clinic
100 West 5th Street, P.O. Box 585
Hamilton, ON L8N 3K7
(905) 575-6014

**Dr. Anthony J. Levitt**
Hamilton Psychiatric Hospital
c/o Mood Disorder Clinic
100 West 5th Street, P.O. Box 585
Hamilton, ON L8N 3K7
(905) 575-6014

**Dr. Meir Steiner**
McMaster Psychiatry Unit
St. Joseph's Hospital
Hamilton, ON L8N 4A6
(416) 522-4941 ext. 3605

**Dr. Virginia Wesson**
Hamilton Psychiatric Hospital
c/o Mood Disorder Clinic
100 West 5th Street, P.O. Box 585
Hamilton, ON L8N 3K7
(905) 575-6014

### Ottawa

**Dr. Margaret Farncombe**
Palliative Care Service
Ottawa Civic Hospital
1053 Carling Avenue
Ottawa, ON K1Y 4E9
(613) 761-4555

**Dr. Edward R. Horn**
Royal Ottawa Hospital
1145 Carling Avenue
Ottawa, ON K1Z 7K4
(613) 724-6500

### London

**Dr. Robert J. M. Lockhart**
1377 Rideau Gate
London, ON N5X 1X2
(519) 642-1627

**Dr. Emmanuel Persad**
850 Highbury Avenue
London, ON N6A 4H1
(519) 455-5110

## Guelph

**Community Mental Health Clinic**
147 Delphi Street
Guelph, ON N1E 4J3
(519) 821-2066
**Dr. Indrajit Ray**
Suite 104, 21 Surrey West
Guelph, ON N1H 3R3
(519) 824-9767

## Other

**Dr. Nancy Armbrust**
38 West Street North
Orillia, ON L3V 5B8
(705) 325-8288
**Dr. Marolyn L. Crewson**
Suite 101, 10425 Kennedy Road N.
Brampton, ON L6T 3S1
(905) 846-7611
**Dr. Kenneth Seaman**
6 - 360 Bayfield Street
Barrie, ON L4M 3C4
(705) 737-1887
**Dr. Laurie Wells**
14 Cross Street
Dundas, ON L9H 2R4
(905) 627-3505

## Quebec

**Dr. Charlene Berger**
574 Roslyn Avenue
Westmount, PQ H3Y 2T8
(514) 485-3970
**Dr. A. Missagh Ghadirian**
Affective Disorder Clinic
1025 Pine Avenue West
Montreal, PQ H3A JA1
(514) 842-1231
**Dr. N.P. Vasavan Nair**
Douglas Hospital Research Center
6875 LaSalle Blvd.
Verdun, PQ H4H 1R3
(514) 761-6131 ext. 23330
**George Schwartz**
Douglas Hospital Research Centre
6875 LaSalle Blvd.
Verdun, PQ H4H 1R3
(514) 761-6131 ext. 3333

## Saskatchewan

**Dr. Dennis G. Bishop**
Box 1089
Rosthern, SK S0K 3R0
(306) 232-4894
**Dr. R.C. Bowen**
Rm. 119 Ellis Hall
Department of Psychiatry
Royal University Hospital
Saskatoon, SK S7N 0W8
(306) 966-8223

# APPENDIX D

# Local Support and Information Groups

This listing should be useful as a starting point in your search for local support groups and sources of further information. However, it is susceptible to change and should not be considered comprehensive. If you know others who should be listed, see "Suggestions and Comments" on page 242.

## UNITED STATES

**Center for Environmental Therapeutics**
Georgetown, CO 80444-0532
(303) 569-0910

**Depression and Related Affective Disorders Association (DRADA)**
Johns Hopkins University School of Medicine
Meyer 3-181
600 North Wolfe Street
Baltimore, MD 21287-7381
(410) 955-4647

**DEPRESSION Awareness Recognition, and Treatment (D/ART) Program**
National Institute of Mental Health
5600 Fishers Lane, Room 10-85
Rockville, MD 20857

**National Depressive and Manic Depressive Association (NMDA)\***
730 North Franklin, #501
Chicago, IL 60610
(800) 826-3632

**Society for Light Treatment and Biological Rhythms**
P.O. Box 478
Wilsonville, OR 97070
(503) 694-2404

## CANADA

### ALBERTA

**Alberta Mental Health Association**
Attn: Margaret Brown
5th Floor, 9942 - 108th Street
Edmonton, AB T5K 2J5
(403) 427-4444

**Canadian Mental Health Association**
Attn: Susan Watson
103, 723 - 14th Street NW
Calgary, AB T2N 2A4
(403) 297-1700

## BRITISH COLUMBIA

**Mood Disorders Association of British Columbia\***
Suite 201
2730 Commercial Drive
Vancouver, BC V5N 5P4
(604) 873-0103
55 Support Groups throughout the province

**Capital Mental Health Association**
125 Skinner Street
Victoria, BC V9A 6X4
(604) 389-1211

**Victoria Mental Health Centre**
(604) 370-5500

**Capital Regional District Mental Health Services**
(604) 952-1629
(604) 356-8163 (all Island)

## MANITOBA

**Mood Disorders Unit**
PZ 202 - PsycHealth Centre
771 Bannatyne Avenue
Winnipeg, MB R3E 3N4
(204) 787-7078

**Society for Depression & Manic Depression**
Winnipeg, MB
(204) 786-0987

**Winnipeg Regional Mental Health Association**
(204) 982-6100

## ONTARIO

**Canadian Mental Health Association**
National Office
2160 Yonge Street
Toronto, ON M4S 2Z3
(416) 484-7750

**Manic-Depressive Association of Metropolitan Toronto\***
Attn: Neasa Martin
40 Orchard View Boulevard, Suite 252
Toronto, ON M4R 1B9
(416) 486-8046

**Self-Help Clearing House of Metropolitan Toronto**
40 Orchard View Blvd., Suite 219
Toronto, ON M4R 1B9
(416) 487-4355

**Edward Szczepan**
SAD Advocacy Group
c/o 371 Morrison Road
Kitchener, ON N2A 2Z5
(519) 893-0462

## PRINCE EDWARD ISLAND

**Mutual Support and Education - Manic Depression**
Attn: Rosemary Faulkner
c/o CMHA
P.O. Box 785
Charlottetown, PEI C1A 7L9

## UNITED KINGDOM

**SADAssociation**
P.O. Box 989
London, United Kingdom
SW7 2PZ

\*Contact to obtain list of support groups in your area.

225

# APPENDIX E

# Light Unit Suppliers

Several types of light therapy equipment are currently on the market, and the number is growing all the time (see pages 228–229). See Chapter 8 for a discussion of each type and the importance of obtaining a unit that adequately protects you from potentially harmful UV radiation. Before purchasing a unit, consult your physician regarding which form of light therapy is most appropriate for you. We have not evaluated the individual products or services. Neither the author nor publisher has any ownership or interest in any of the light unit suppliers.

### Apria Health Care

6040 North Cutter Circle
Portland, OR 97217
(503) 735-0200

### Apollo Light Systems

352 West 1060 South
Orem, UT 84058
(801) 226-2370

### Bio-Brite, Inc.

7315 Wisconsin Avenue
Besthesda, MD 20814-3202
1-800 621-5483

### Crisis Management Resources

Suite 600, 250 - 6th Avenue SW
Calgary, AB, Canada T2P 3H7
(403) 263-2200

### DayLight Technologies, Inc.

Box 102, CRO
Halifax, NS B3J 2L4
(902) 422-0804
1-800-387-0896

### ELC (Environmental Lighting Consultants)

3923 Coconut Palm Drive, Suite 101
Tampa, FL 33619
(813) 621-0058
1-800-842-8848

### Enviro-Med

1600 SE - 141st Avenue
Vancouver, WA 98684
(206) 256-6989
1-800-222-3296

### Health Light, Inc.

P.O. Box 3899, Station C
Hamilton, ON L8H 7P2
(905) 545-4997

### Hughes Lighting Technologies

34 Yacht Club Drive
Lake Hapatcong, NJ 07849
(201) 663-1214

### Lighting Resources

1421 West Third Avenue
Columbus, OH 43212-2928
(614) 488-6841

### Lighting Specialities

78 NW Couch
Portland, OR 97209
(503) 226-3461

### Medlight

Avon, MA
1-800-453-4633 (US)

### Northern Light Technology

3070 Brabaet-Marineau
St. Laurent, PQ H4S 1K7
(514) 335-1763
1-800-263-0066

### Pi Square, Inc.

11036 - 1st Avenue SW
Seattle, WA 98168-1402
1-800-786-3296

### Sphere One, Inc.

432 Main Street, POB 9
Silver Plume, CO 80476
(201) 942-9772

### The SunBox Company

19217 Orbit Drive
Gaithersburg, MD 20879
1-800-548-3968

### SUNNEX Biotechnologies, Inc.

1200 - 191 Lombard Avenue
Winnipeg, MB R3B 0X1
(204) 956-2476

### VitalAire

VitalAire (formerly ARS VitalAire)
has over 60 offices in Canada.
Consult your telephone
directory, or in Central and
Eastern Canada contact 1-905-
949-5444 and in Western
Canada contact 1-403-944-0202.

### Winter Sun Lighting

P.O. Box 15121
Portland, OR 97215
(503) 233-1206

### Wolff Systems Tech

Norcross, GA
(404) 242-9807 (fax)

| Supplier Outlets | Light Boxes | Desk Lamps | Visors/ Caps | Dawn Simulators |
|---|---|---|---|---|
| **UNITED STATES** | | | | |
| *Florida* | | | | |
| Environmental Lighting Concepts | Yes | | | |
| *Georgia* | | | | |
| Wolff Systems Tech | Yes | | | |
| *Maryland* | | | | |
| Bio-Brite | Yes | | Yes | Yes |
| Pi Square | Yes | Yes | | Yes |
| The SunBox Company | Yes | Yes | Yes | Yes |
| *Massachusetts* | | | | |
| Medlight | Yes | | | |
| *New Jersey* | | | | |
| Hughes Lighting Technologies | Yes | Yes | | Yes |
| Sphere One, Inc. | Yes | Yes | | Yes |
| (Also supplies UV filter mentioned on page 132.) | | | | |
| *Ohio* | | | | |
| Lighting Resources | Yes | Yes | Yes | Yes |
| *Oregon* | | | | |
| Apria Health Care | Yes | | | |
| Lighting Specialties | Yes | Yes | | |
| Winter Sun Lighting | Yes | Yes | | Yes |

| Supplier Outlets | Light Boxes | Desk Lamps | Visors/ Caps | Dawn Simulators |
|---|---|---|---|---|
| *Utah* | | | | |
| Apollo Light Systems | Yes | | | |
| *Washington* | | | | |
| Enviro-Med | Yes | Yes | | Yes |
| **CANADA** | | | | |
| *Alberta* | | | | |
| Crisis Management Resources | | | | Yes |
| VitalAire | Yes | | Yes | Yes |
| *British Columbia* | | | | |
| VitalAire | Yes | | Yes | Yes |
| *Manitoba* | | | | |
| Sunnex Biotechnologies | | Yes | | |
| VitalAire | Yes | | Yes | Yes |
| *Ontario* | | | | |
| Health Light | | | Yes | |
| VitalAire | Yes | | Yes | Yes |
| *Quebec* | | | | |
| Northern Light Technologies | | Yes | | |
| VitalAire | Yes | | Yes | Yes |
| *Nova Scotia* | | | | |
| DayLight Technologies | Yes | Yes | | Yes |
| (Also supplies UV filter mentioned on page 132.) | | | | |
| VitalAire | Yes | | Yes | Yes |

# APPENDIX F

# The Columbia Eye Check-up for Users of Light Treatment

See "Before You Undertake Light Therapy" (page 108).

Patient _____     Examined by _____
Address _____     Address _____
        _____             _____
        _____             _____
Phone _____        Phone _____
Referred by _____  Date of exam _____

## CHECKLIST

RETINA

| | |
|---|---|
| Detachment | + - |
| Diabetic retinopathy | + - |
| Retinal vasculitis/Chorioretinal inflammation | + - |
| Vascular retinopathies | + - |
| Central serous retinopathy | + - |
| Degenerative disease of the macula | + - |
| Tapeto-retinal degenerations | + - |
| Solar/radiation retinopathy | + - |
| Drug-induced retinopathy | + - |
| Post-traumatic retinopathy | + - |

EYE COMPLAINTS

| | |
|---|---|
| Photophobia | + - |
| Glare | + - |
| Dry eyes | + - |
| Blurred vision | + - |
| Metamorphopsia | + - |
| Color vision (poor, good) | + - |
| Night vision (poor, good) | + - |
| Other complaints: | |

OTHER

| | |
|---|---|
| Inflammatory diseases of anterior segment/uveal tract | + - |
| Glaucoma | + - |
| Cataracts | + - |
| Optic nerve affections | + - |
| Keratoconjunctivitis sicca | + - |
| Hypothyroidism | + - |
| hormone supplement (yes, no) | + - |
| stable (yes, no) | + - |

CURRENT MEDICATIONS

| | |
|---|---|
| Antidepressants (tricyclic) | + - |
| Neuroleptics (phenothiazine) | + - |
| Lithium | + - |
| Tryptophan or melatonin | + - |
| Psoralens | + - |
| Antimalarial/antirheumatics | + - |
| Diuretics (hydrochlorothiazide) | + - |
| Porphyrins | + - |
| Tetracycline | + - |
| Sulfonamides | + - |
| Other photosensitizers: | |

230

## EXAMINATION

*Best corrected visual acuity*

      R         L

$V_{SC}$ _____ _____

$V_{CC}$ _____ _____    Wearing   _____

                                            _____

*Ocular motility (9 cardinal directions of gaze)*

      R                                     L

*Intraocular pressure (applanation), noting time of day:*   _____

     R _____             L _____

---

Note: Examining doctor should include a summary note indicating any problematic ocular conditions. This set of ocular tests was specified for patients in the Clinical Chronobiology Program at the New York State Psychiatric Institute, Columbia-Presbyterian Medical Center. The development team included: Pamela F. Gallin, M.D., Brian Rafferty, A.B., and Michael Terman, Ph.D., of Columbia University; Ronald M. Burde, M.D., of the Albert Einstein College of Medicine; and Charlotte E. Remé, M.D., of the University of Zürich, Switzerland. August 1993 version. © 1993, New York State Psychiatric Institute. For further information, see: Terman, M. et al. (1990) *Photochemistry and Photobiology* **51**: 781–791.

## *Amsler grid*

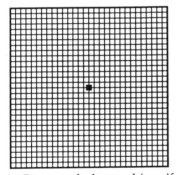 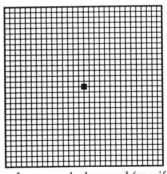

   R   normal, abnormal (specify)          L   normal, abnormal (specify)

*Pupillary reactions*

| R | | | | L | | |
|---|---|---|---|---|---|---|
| direct | + | - | | direct | + | - |
| indirect | + | - | | indirect | + | - |

*Slit lamp examination*

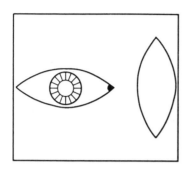

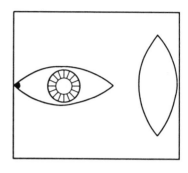

R                                              L

*Ocular fundus* (direct ___ / indirect ___ / mydriasis ___)

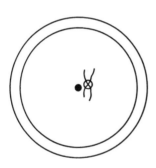

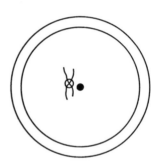

R c/d = _____                    R c/d = _____

# INDEX

# BOOKS AVAILABLE FROM SCRIPT PUBLISHING INC.

## SCRIPT: GOOD HEALTH BOOKS

- **Fight the Winter Blues, Don't Be SAD:**
  **Your Guide to Conquering Seasonal Affective Disorder,**
  by Celeste A. Peters          ISBN 1-896015-01-8   ($18.95)
  As winter approaches, do you become depressed, lose control of
  your appetite, crave starchy and sweet foods, feel incredibly
  fatigued or unable to get enough sleep? If this sounds like you or
  someone you know, this book can be a valuable guide out of the
  dark days of winter.

- **Parenting Today's Teenager Effectively:**
  **Hear Me, Hug Me, Trust Me,**
  by Dr. G. Scott Wooding          ISBN 1-896015-03-4   ($18.95)
  Hear Me, Hug Me, Trust Me are the main principles behind an
  approach to effective parenting that stresses listening to teens, even
  in disciplinary situations; showing them that you love them, even
  when they make mistakes; and giving them freedom to try new
  things.

- **Taking Control of Your Blood Pressure:**
  **Steps to a Healthier Lifestyle,**
  by Lorna Milkovich, Beverly          ISBN 0-9694287-4-X
  Whitmore & Peter Henderson, Ph.D.          ($16.95)
  A workbook written for people with high blood pressure. You can:
  - assess your own lifestyle
  - learn how your lifestyle affects your blood pressure
  - learn how to control weight, eat a balanced diet, manage stress,
    quit smoking, and exercise safely
  - learn how blood pressure medication works
  Written by health professionals working in a hypertension clinic.
  Start taking an active role in your treatment today.

- **Choices—When Your Child Is Dying,**
  by Sheila A. Lee          ISBN 1-896015-04-2   ($14.95)
  A sensitive and informative guide on how to cope and make the
  best decisions when your child is dying.

*SEE ORDER FORM ON PAGE 240.*

## SCRIPT: GOOD QUESTION BOOKS

edited by Ty Reynolds, illustrated by Robert Jobst

Canada's most popular trivia books (over 100,000 in print). Over 500 questions and answers and 60 cartoon illustrations in the series. These books make great bathroom reading, get-well gifts and travel companions. A must for trivia buffs. (#s 1-5: $8.95 each; #6: $9.95 each) Titles include:

- **That's a Good Question 6**     ISBN 1-896015-02-6
- **Who on Earth is Dr. Pepper?**     ISBN 1-896015-00-X
- **Why do Golfers Yell Fore?**     ISBN 0-9694287-7-4
- **What the Heck is a Grape Nut?**     ISBN 0-9694287-6-6
- **That's a Good Question Canada!**     ISBN 0-9694287-2-3
- **That's a Good Question!**     ISBN 0-9694287-0-7

## SCRIPT: THE WRITERS' GROUP

*Business & Sports*
- **It's How You Play the Game:**
  **The Inside Story of the Calgary Winter Olympics,**
  by Frank King, foreword by Juan Antonio Samaranch
         ISBN 0-9694287-5-8, hardcover ($24.95)

A gripping, entertaining and emotional account written by the chairman of the Calgary Olympic Organizing Committee. This 376-page hardcover book is beautifully illustrated with 32 pages of colour photographs. It chronicles the amazing power of people inspired by the Olympic spirit to achieve what defeatists thought impossible.

*Biography*
- **Hawrelak: The Story,**     ISBN 0-9694287-8-2
  by Diane Stuemer            ($16.95)

## ORDER INFORMATION

**Payment**   Complete payment must accompany your order. Make checks payable to Script Publishing Inc.

**Shipping**   Allow four to six weeks delivery. Books are sent by surface mail, usually within 24 hours of receipt of order.

*SEE ORDER FORM ON PAGE 240.*

# ORDER FORM

| BOOK TITLE | | PRICE* | NO. OF COPIES | TOTAL COST |
|---|---|---|---|---|
| Fight the Winter Blues, | U.S. $: | 14.95 | | |
| Don't Be SAD | Cdn. $: | 18.95 | | |
| Parenting Today's Teenager: | U.S. $: | 14.95 | | |
| Hear Me, Hug Me, Trust Me | Cdn. $: | 18.95 | | |
| Choices—When Your Child Is Dying | | 14.95 | | |
| Taking Control of Your Blood Pressure | | 16.95 | | |
| *Good Question books:* | | | | |
| That's a Good Question 6 | | 9.95 | | |
| Who on Earth is Dr. Pepper? | | 8.95 | | |
| Why do Golfers Yell Fore? | | 8.95 | | |
| What the Heck is a Grape Nut? | | 8.95 | | |
| That's a Good Question Canada! | | 8.95 | | |
| That's a Good Question! | | 8.95 | | |
| It's How You Play the Game | | 24.95 | | |
| Hawrelak: The Story | | 16.95 | | |

| **SHIPPING COSTS | | | |
|---|---|---|---|
| Value of Order | Shipping Costs | | |
| 8.95 – 35.00 | 4.00 | | |
| 35.00 – 70.00 | 8.00 | | |
| 70.00 – 100.00 | 10.00 | | |
| 100.00 + | 12.00 | | |

| | |
|---|---|
| Books Total Price | |
| Shipping Costs** | |
| Canadian orders only add GST | |
| Grand Total | |

*USA orders remit in US funds. (Prices subject to change without notice.)

**Please complete payment and shipping information on the next page.**

## METHOD OF PAYMENT

❑ Check   ❑ Money order   ❑ VISA
(Payment by check must be guaranteed by a credit card, or
your order will not be shipped until your check clears.)

Credit card number _____

Name on card _____ Exp. date ____/____

## SHIPPING LABEL

Please print clearly — this will be used as your shipping label.
(Allow 4–6 weeks for delivery)

Send books to:

Name _____

Organization _____

Street Address _____

City _____   Prov/State _____

Postal/Zip Code _____   Country _____

Telephone (_____) _____

## FAX, PHONE OR MAIL YOUR ORDER TODAY TO

Script Publishing Inc.
Suite 200, 839 - 5th Avenue S.W.
Calgary, Alberta T2P 3C8
Ph. (403) 290-0800
Fax (403) 241-8575

241

## SUGGESTIONS AND COMMENTS

### WE WOULD LIKE TO HEAR FROM YOU

If you have a SAD story you would like to share or any comments about this book and how we can make it better, please write to the publisher, Script Publishing Inc., at the address below. Feel free to use the accompanying form.

If you are a health care professional working in a clinic or in research with SAD sufferers, a light supplier, or a representative of a SAD support group and your name is not yet in the appendices, please tell us who you are, where you are located, and what you do.

#### *Script Publishing Inc.*
Suite 200, 839 - 5th Avenue S.W., Calgary, Alberta, Canada T2P 3C8
Phone (403) 290-0800  Fax (403) 241-8575

### COMMENTS

_____

_____

_____

_____

_____

_____

_____

_____

Name _____

Street/P.O. Box _____

| City/ Town | Province/ State | Postal Code/Zip |
|---|---|---|

Do you suffer from SAD or Winter Blues? _____

How long have you suffered? _____ Age \_\_\_\_ Sex \_\_\_\_

## PERMISSIONS

Thanks to the National Institute of Mental Health, Bethesda, Maryland, for permission to adapt and reproduce the *Seasonal Pattern Assessment Questionnaire* authored by Dr. Norman Rosenthal, Dr. Gary J. Bradt and Dr. Thomas A. Wehr; to New York State Psychiatric Institute for permission to reprint *The Columbia Eye Check-up for Users of Light Therapy* and *How to use the Amsler Grid*; to The Guilford Press for permission to adapt and reproduce graphs from the article *On the Question of Mechanism in Phototherapy for Seasonal Affective Disorder: Considerations of Clinical Efficacy and Epidemiology* by Dr. Michael Terman; to Key Porter Books Limited for permission to reprint selected recipes from *The Lighthearted Cookbook* by Anne Lindsay; and to Canadian Western Natural Gas Blue Flame Kitchen for permission to reprint *Freezing Tips*.